CAMPAIGN 338

THE FIRST ANGLO-SIKH WAR 1845–46

The betrayal of the *Khalsa*

DAVID SMITH

ILLUSTRATED BY STEVE NOON
Series editor Marcus Cowper

OSPREY PUBLISHING
Bloomsbury Publishing Plc
PO Box 883, Oxford, OX1 9PL, UK
1385 Broadway, 5th Floor, New York, NY 10018, USA
E-mail: info@ospreypublishing.com
www.ospreypublishing.com

OSPREY is a trademark of Osprey Publishing Ltd

First published in Great Britain in 2019

A catalogue record for this book is available from the British Library.

ISBN: PB: 978 1 4728 3447 8
           ePub: 978 1 4728 3446 1
           ePDF: 978 1 4728 3445 4
           XML: 978 1 4728 3448 5

19 20 21 22 23   10 9 8 7 6 5 4 3 2 1

Index by Fionbar Lyons
Typeset in Myriad Pro and Sabon
Maps by Bounford.com
3D BEVs by The Black Spot
Page layouts by PDQ Digital Media Solutions, Bungay, UK
Printed in China through World Print Ltd.

Artist's note

Readers may care to note that the original paintings from which the colour
plates in this book were prepared are available for private sale. All
reproduction copyright whatsoever is retained by the Publishers. The artist
can be contacted via the following website:

www.steve-noon.co.uk

The Publishers regret that they can enter into no correspondence upon
this matter.

Osprey Publishing supports the Woodland Trust, the UK's leading woodland
conservation charity.

To find out more about our authors and books visit
www.ospreypublishing.com. Here you will find extracts, author
interviews, details of forthcoming events and the option to sign up for
our newsletter.

Acknowledgements

I would like to thank various people for their help in the preparation of this
book: Peter Harrington for permission to use images from the Anne S. K.
Brown Military Collection at Brown University Library, and Marcus Cowper
and Nikolai Bogdanovic for their help and support during the
production process.

Dedication

This book is dedicated to my family – Shirley, Harry and Josh.

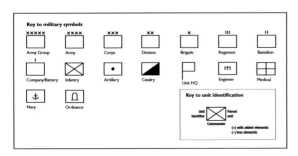

CONTENTS

British control over India prior to the First Anglo-Sikh War

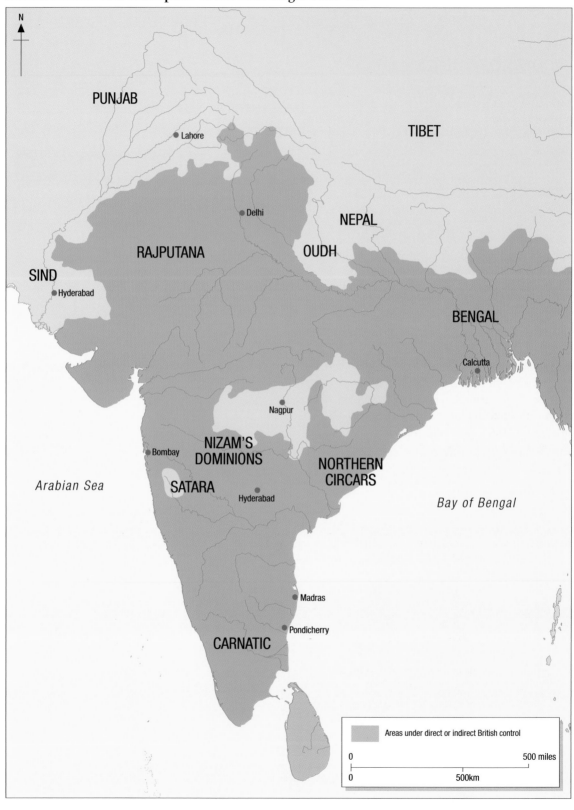

ORIGINS OF THE CAMPAIGN

The First Anglo-Sikh War is quite possibly unique, inasmuch as both sides entered into hostilities with exactly the same aim. Both the ruling aristocracy of the Sikh state and the British, in the form of the East India Company, entered the war with the primary goal of destroying the Sikh Army. The British saw it as a serious threat to their growing dominance over India, while the rulers of the Sikh state saw it as a threat to their very existence.

Ranjit Singh, the driving force behind the solidification and expansion of the Sikh state, foresaw trouble with the army of the East India Company and developed his army accordingly. (IndiaPictures/UIG via Getty Images)

The great Sikh Maharajah Ranjit Singh is said to have gazed upon a map of India, noting the areas shaded red to denote their control by the East India Company, and to have commented, 'one day it will all be red'. If this is more than mere legend, then this could be seen as the first step towards war with the British. The historian Amarpal Singh has termed the conflict an 'inevitable trial of strength between the two powers', but it only became inevitable after Ranjit Singh's death. Prior to that, he was both the driving force in the expansion of the Sikh Army, and the only person capable of controlling it.

The collapse of the Mughal Empire, by the end of the previous century, had left a number of kings and princes in control of various regions. The East India Company, exploiting political divisions and disunity among the Indian states, as well as the superior discipline of its own army, began to assume control over large swathes of the country until Kashmir, the Punjab and Sind were left as the main independent regions. In the Punjab, states known as *misls* were successful in expelling their Afghan controllers, but although they could work together against a common foe, they also continually squabbled among each other for control of resources and territory and were unable to coalesce into a unified state. The emergence of Ranjit Singh changed this situation, as he had the personality and political ability to unite the Sikhs under his rule. After declaring himself maharajah in 1801, he set about pulling the disunited *misls* together.

Trouble may well have erupted earlier, as Ranjit Singh had ambitions to expand his empire south of the Sutlej River, but the Treaty of Amritsar of 1809 (which recognized British control of this region) calmed the situation. Indeed, the British were happy to have a settled, unified Sikh state to act as a buffer between their own dominions and the troublesome regions to the north. The period of good relations between the Sikhs and the British also allowed Ranjit Singh to continue with his consolidation of the Sikh state, but the East India Company was still viewed as a potential future rival. Ranjit Singh therefore embarked upon a series of reforms to his army, specifically designed to counter British forces.

Sikh military tradition placed cavalry at the heart of the army, but Ranjit Singh had noted how disciplined infantry repeatedly won the day for the British. He therefore tipped the traditional hierarchy on its head and made the infantry the elite of his army. A powerful artillery force backed up these foot soldiers, with the cavalry reduced to a secondary role. European drill was introduced, and foreign officers were welcomed to instil discipline.

By the time Ranjit Singh died, on 27 June 1839, the Sikh Army was a formidable force and a clear challenger to the East India Company should anyone wish to point it in that direction. An infantry contingent of 47,000 was supplemented by 16,000 cavalry and almost 500 guns of various calibres. An army on such a scale placed a huge strain on the empire's finances and only continued expansion of the Sikh state could support this. The limit on Sikh expansion imposed by the British was therefore an important element in the unrest that was to come. More important, however, was the death of Ranjit Singh, which plunged the state into chaos. Shorn of their powerful

Under military commanders like Robert Clive (depicted here at the Siege of Arcot in 1751, in a painting by Ernest Wallcousins), the East India Company steadily exploited the power vacuum left by the collapse of the Mughal Empire.

leader, rival factions fell into bickering over the succession and a series of ineffectual rulers took turns to deepen the crisis. In fact, exactly the sort of political infighting that the British had been able to exploit in other regions of the country now fragmented the Sikh state, making it simultaneously a more vulnerable target for the British to consider and a cause for concern.

The Sikh court split into rival powers, the Dogra and Sikh factions, with the former built on a trio of Hindu brothers and the latter on the Sikh aristocracy itself, known as the *Khalsa*. The army, also often referred to as the *Khalsa*, saw an opportunity in this rivalry and began to play one side against the other, forcing the factions to court favour with the powerful armed forces of the state. As the soldiers continued to extort ever-higher wages from aspirants to the throne, payment became difficult if not impossible and disciple began to break down. Open defiance, the occasional murder of unpopular officers and even the looting of the civilian population became common. The British, with their hands full in Afghanistan, nevertheless noted with concern the growing instability in the Punjab.

The Tripartite Treaty of 1838, part of Britain's interests in installing a puppet government in Afghanistan, had meant that Sikh soldiers actually fought alongside the British in that country. One general to earn distinction in this manner, Nao Nihal Singh, was the son of the ineffective Maharajah Kharak Singh (one of Ranjit Singh's seven sons and his designated successor). Nao Nihal Singh used his military prowess and good relationship with the British to take over the state from his father, and for a while it looked as if firm rule had been restored. In November 1840, a freak accident (some suspected foul play) returned the state to chaos: Nao Nihal Singh was killed by a falling beam while walking under an archway following his father's funeral. Rival factions again formed behind two candidates for the throne. Sher Singh, another of Ranjit Singh's sons, was popular with the British, but it was Kharak Singh's widow, Chand Kaur, who was made maharani (empress), on 2 December 1840. A rather unpolished character, ill-equipped for the diplomatic duties her new position entailed, she was an unpopular ruler, despite being known as the *Mai* (mother).

Sher Singh was unwilling to accept this situation and began to actively undermine the Maharani. His principle method for achieving this was to promise higher wages to soldiers in the Sikh Army, which prompted many to desert to his camp. The British were uncomfortable with this development, and the growing instability it fostered, but were still preoccupied in Afghanistan. Recognizing Sher Singh as pro-British, support was therefore given to his bid for power. Emboldened, Sher Singh marched on Lahore, the seat of the Durbar (court), panicking the Maharani into offering lavish gifts to her remaining soldiers. Although happy to accept the gifts, the men recognized her actions as a symptom of fear and weakness, and continued to desert. By the time hostilities broke out, in January 1841, Sher Singh had 26,000 soldiers compared to just 5,000 for the Maharani, and two days of battle were enough to bring about the inevitable surrender. Chand Kaur had ruled for less than two months.

On 27 January 1841, Sher Singh was installed as maharajah, but he almost immediately got into difficulties with the army. Unable to make good on the extravagant promises he had made to win their support, he lost the confidence of the soldiers, who ransacked the bazaars of Lahore and became ungovernable. A weak effort at negotiation ended in capitulation,

Ranjit Singh welcomed foreign mercenaries and advisors to his court, aware that he needed to model his new army on the disciplined forces of Europe. (Universal History Archive/UIG via Getty Images)

as Sher Singh effectively told the army to sort matters out for themselves, while he retreated into a life of dissipation, drawing comfort from drink and women and turning a blind eye to the unravelling of his state.

The British, however, were unable to turn a blind eye. Seeing that Sher Singh was not the strong, anglophile leader they had banked on, their attitude towards the Punjab became steadily more hostile. In particular, the volatility of the Sikh Army was of concern. Left to govern itself, its men elected officers (*pances*) to sit in councils (*panchayats*) to debate orders. Inevitably, the desire to be elected led to officers making promises regarding wages and other perks, so able politicians and the unscrupulous ascended into positions of influence in the army, rather than those with competence in military matters.

Equally alarming was the expansionist policy followed by the Dogra faction, who pushed forces into Tibet. A strong buffer state had been an agreeable prospect for the British, but an aggressive and expanding Sikh Empire was not what they had in mind. Although operations in Tibet ultimately went badly (a Sikh army was destroyed at Tuklakote in December 1841), they had secured dazzling success prior to that, raising British eyebrows.

The Sikhs were still helping Britain with operations in Afghanistan, but the relationship was definitely cooling. The British, in fact, had been surprised by the strength of support offered by the Punjab, believing them to be unreliable at best. Despite this, the Tripartite Treaty was unceremoniously scrapped once it had served its purpose, much to the disgust of the Sikhs, who felt they had been used as far as they could help the British and then casually discarded without any warning.

In 1843, British forces under General Charles Napier effected a conquest of Sind. Although taking over the state far exceeded Napier's orders (he was still rewarded with a knighthood), this was seen by the Sikhs as more evidence of British expansionism. More worrying was British support for a Sikh faction, the Sandhawalia clan, who were both pro-British and anti-Dogra. In particular, they were vehemently opposed to Sher Singh's chief minister, Dhian Singh Dogra. The situation culminated in an orgy of bloodletting, as Sandhawalia elements murdered Sher Singh, his son Pratap Singh and Dhian Singh Dogra, before in turn being butchered by a vengeful Sikh Army. This shocking display of violence resulted in Dalip Singh, youngest acknowledged son of Ranjit Singh, attaining the throne.

The Punjab and surrounding regions

1. The 1809 treaty between the Sikh Empire and Britain recognizes British control over areas to the south of the Sutlej.
2. Tripartite agreement of 1838 states that Shah Soojah is the rightful ruler of Afghanistan. He accepts Sikh rule of former Afghan provinces conquered by Ranjit Singh but will receive help from the Sikhs and the British to gain control of Afghanistan.
3. First Afghan War, 1839–42. British army destroyed during retreat from Kabul.
4. 1843: Charles Napier controversially conquers Sind, having been dispatched there with a Bombay Presidency army to quell rebel activity.

Dalip Singh faced immediate challenges from a pair of ambitious stepbrothers and, being just 7 years of age, was unable to fend for himself. His mother, Jind Jaur (also known as Jindan), therefore took on the role of regent, and also elevated her brother, Jawahar Singh, into the Lahore court. With the situation volatile, and the massive army (numbering close to 70,000 infantry at this stage) barely under control, British observers began to anticipate a call for assistance from the ruling class. Consequently, troops began to be moved closer to the Sutlej, which did nothing to calm the situation. There is also evidence that the British were by now looking for war, or at least believing that it was inevitable. Some wealthy families began to leave the region, others began to petition the British for protection and guarantees that they could retain their land in the event that the East India Company took over the state.

Sir Henry Hardinge, who had arrived in India to take up the position of governor general in July 1844, began an active campaign to weaken the Sikh state, and Major George Broadfoot, installed as agent for the north-west frontier in October, was an undiplomatic character who sometimes acted with open hostility to the Sikhs. Tension inevitably increased as trust on both sides was eroded, but it was not yet considered time to go to war. Acting under the misapprehension that they would be able to decide when hostilities should commence, British forces began their slow preparations. A flotilla of boats, which could be used to construct a pontoon bridge for crossing the Sutlej, was provocatively assembled near Ferozepore, under the transparent cover of being intended for the transport of grain.

Sher Singh was both pro-British and a seemingly strong character. As such, he appeared to be the ideal man to restore order to the Sikh Empire, but once in power he quickly showed his true colours. (Fine Art Photographic Library/CORBIS/Corbis via Getty Images)

Troops were dispersed over a wide area, however, and it would take time for them to be brought together into an effective army, but plans were set in place to make mobilization as rapid as possible once the decision was made to go to war. Opinion is divided on how keenly the British sought an armed confrontation, but many people saw it as a certainty, whether it was desirable or not. A newspaper article from Sir Charles Napier, in the *Delhi Gazette*, inflamed the situation, as he wrote that a British invasion of the Punjab was inevitable.

With the Sikh Army now a menace to its own people as troops rampaged through villages and towns, the situation had reached boiling point. The common soldiers held all the power, as they elected their own officers, so there was no way of bringing the army to heel. As many as three-quarters of the men were absent without leave on any given day, either attending to personal business or simply looting. Training was almost completely neglected.

For a brief period, the Sikh forces were turned on themselves, as units marched on Jammu to confront the controversial Raja Gulab Singh and bring him to Lahore. Having avoided travelling to the capital as much as possible (he had been lucky to escape with his life after commanding the forces of Maharani Chand Kaur during her confrontation with Sher Singh), he must have feared that his run was over, but he managed to cajole the soldiery and returned to Jammu. Once there, he immediately began offering his support to the British, who at first refused to acknowledge his approaches. Wanting to establish an independent Dogra state, Gulab Singh asked only for territories in the north of the Sikh Empire (in which the British had no interest) in return for holding his own army out of any conflict. The situation was awkward, but the possibility of removing Gulab Singh from the military equation, for such a reasonable price, was obviously intriguing for the British.

Frantic manoeuvrings on the part of the rivals for the seat of power led to the death of the army's favourite candidate to rule the state, Peshaura Singh. Holding Jawahar Singh responsible, the *Khalsa* murdered the *vizier*, an act for which his sister, Jindan, swore she would have her revenge. The position of *vizier* was then offered by the *Khalsa* (firmly establishing them as the dominant power in the state) to Gulab Singh, who tartly replied that he would prefer to live for longer than six months. Lal Singh, the lover of Jindan, was thus thrust into the position of *vizier*.

Jind Kaur, or Jindan, was a powerful figure at the Sikh court following the accession to the throne of her 7-year-old son, Dalip Singh. Painting by George Richmond.

Having been created initially to challenge the supremacy of the East India Company forces, the *Khalsa* was naturally anti-British in sentiment. Aggression towards the East India Company was more or less in the Sikh Army's DNA, and the British politicians, including Broadfoot and Hardinge, sensed that the time for negotiation had passed. It was still hoped that the Sikhs would not cross the Sutlej, at least not until the East India Company had gathered its strength for the struggle that would follow such a move, but events took on their own momentum and, on 13 December, Hardinge was informed that just such a crossing had taken place. The British were not ready, but preparations were under way. They had not been caught completely off-guard, but even so, the Sikh Army would present a serious challenge.

Elements on both sides – the ruling elite in the Punjab and the British themselves – had come to view as intolerable the Sikh Army's position of dominance. Both sides now had the same goal. 'This would be no war of conquest,' noted Amarpal Singh, 'but one organised specifically to annihilate the recalcitrant Sikh army.'

CHRONOLOGY

1801	Ranjit Singh declares himself maharajah.
*c.*1805	Reforms to the Sikh Army begin, with European practices (first British and later French) being the model.
1809	Treaty of Amritsar grants the British control over areas south of the Sutlej.
1838	June: Tripartite Treaty between Britain, Ranjit Singh and Shah Soojah, intended to install Shah Soojah as a puppet ruler in Afghanistan.
1839	March: First Anglo-Afghan War begins.
	27 June: Ranjit Singh dies.
1840	November: Death of Kharak Singh and, shortly after, his son Nao Nihal Singh.
	2 December: Chand Kaur proclaimed maharani.
1841	27 January: Sher Singh becomes maharajah, seizing power from Maharani Chand Kaur, but almost immediately begins to lose control of the army.
1842	6 January: In Afghanistan, British forces begin the retreat from Kabul.
1843	17 February: Battle of Miani, in Sind, results in a victory for Charles Napier.
	24 March: Battle of Hyderabad. Victory for Napier leads to the annexation of Sind.
	15 September: Sher Singh, his son Pratap Singh and his chief minister Dhian Singh Dogra murdered by Sandhawalia elements.
1844	22 July: Sir Henry Hardinge arrives in India to take up the position of Governor General, replacing Lord Ellenborough.
	October: Major George Broadfoot installed as agent for the north-west frontier, based at Ludhiana.
1845	21 September: Jawahar Singh killed by the *Khalsa*.
	3 December: Diplomatic relations with Lahore broken off.
	11 December: Sikhs cross the Sutlej, with one corps threatening Ferozepore and another basing itself at Ferozeshah.
	13 December: British declare war on the Sikhs.
	18 December: Battle of Mudki.
	21 December: Battle of Ferozeshah (first day).
	22 December: Battle of Ferozeshah (second day).

1846	6 January: 10,000 reinforcements under Sir John Grey reach Sir Hugh Gough.
	17 January: Ranjodh Singh crosses the Sutlej with around 10,000 men. Sir Harry Smith captures Sikh-held forts at Futteyghur and Dhurmcote.
	21 January: Smith's column bombarded by Sikh guns while passing Bhudowal.
	28 January: The Battle of Aliwal, the 'battle without a mistake'.
	10 February: The Battle of Sobraon effectively ends the war.
	10 February: The British begin to cross the Sutlej at Attaree Ford.
	16 February: Gulab Singh reaches the British camp and opens peace negotiations.
	19 February: The British reach Lahore.
	9 March: The Treaty of Lahore. Jullunder Doab and Kashmir handed over to British control, as well as Sikh lands south of the Sutlej. War reparations of 6 million rupees extracted.
	16 March: Treaty of Amritsar formalizes the arrangement with Gulab Singh. Kashmir is handed over in return for 7.5 million rupees.
	26 December: The Treaty of Bhyroval. British Resident is installed in Lahore.
1848	18 April: The Second Anglo-Sikh War begins.
	22 November: The Battle of Ramnagar.
1849	13 January: The Battle of Chillianwala. Heavy British casualties lead to Gough being replaced as commander-in-chief, but his replacement, Sir Charles Napier, does not arrive in time to take command before the final battle of the war.
	21 February: The Battle of Gujerat. Gough restores his reputation somewhat with a comprehensive victory.
1863	1 August: Jind Kaur dies in exile, but her body is returned to India for cremation.
1893	22 October: Dalip Singh, the last maharajah of the Sikh Empire, dies in exile. He is given a Christian burial in Elveden.

OPPOSING COMMANDERS

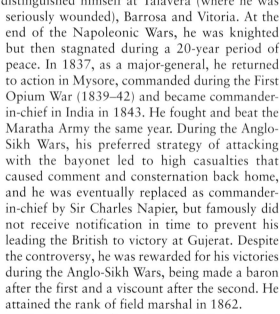

BRITISH

Sir Hugh Gough (1779–1869), commander-in-chief in India. The son of a militia officer, the army was always a likely destination for Gough, who got his commission at the age of 13. He gained his first experience at the Cape of Good Hope and in the West Indies, but his reputation was made in the Peninsular War under the Duke of Wellington. As a major commanding the Royal Irish Fusiliers, he distinguished himself at Talavera (where he was seriously wounded), Barrosa and Vitoria. At the end of the Napoleonic Wars, he was knighted but then stagnated during a 20-year period of peace. In 1837, as a major-general, he returned to action in Mysore, commanded during the First Opium War (1839–42) and became commander-in-chief in India in 1843. He fought and beat the Maratha Army the same year. During the Anglo-Sikh Wars, his preferred strategy of attacking with the bayonet led to high casualties that caused comment and consternation back home, and he was eventually replaced as commander-in-chief by Sir Charles Napier, but famously did not receive notification in time to prevent his leading the British to victory at Gujerat. Despite the controversy, he was rewarded for his victories during the Anglo-Sikh Wars, being made a baron after the first and a viscount after the second. He attained the rank of field marshal in 1862.

Sir Henry Hardinge (1785–1856), Governor General and Lieutenant-General. Although primarily a political figure during the First Anglo-Sikh War, Hardinge was a man of vast military experience, making his offer to act as Sir Hugh Gough's second-in-command at Ferozeshah perfectly reasonable. Starting out as an ensign in the Queen's Rangers in 1799, he climbed through the ranks, moving from one regiment to the next, before attending the Royal Military College in

1806. Hardinge was credited with turning the tide during the Battle of Albuera in 1811 (a fact he referred to during the desperate night following the first day's fighting at Ferozeshah) and was knighted in 1814. Seriously wounded when fighting alongside the Prussians at Ligny in 1815 (he lost his left hand), he was presented one of Napoleon's swords by the Duke of Wellington. From 1820, Hardinge served as a member of parliament and as secretary of war under both Wellington and Sir Robert Peel, before taking over from Lord Ellenborough as Governor General of India, in 1844. Following the First Anglo-Sikh War, he was made Viscount Hardinge of Lahore. Back in England, he became commander-in-chief of the British Army in 1852 and was responsible for the direction of the Crimean War.

Sir Harry Smith (1787–1860), Major-General. One of 11 children, Henry Smith (always known as 'Harry') served in the Whittlesea troop of Yeoman Cavalry in 1804, at the age of 16. He first caught the eye at the Battle of Montevideo, in 1807, where he played a conspicuous role in the storming of a narrow breach in the city walls. During the Napoleonic Wars, he saw action with the 95th Rifles, and in 1812, following the storming of Badajoz, was introduced to the 14-year-old girl who would become his wife. A spell in the United States allowed him to witness the burning of the White House in 1814, before he returned to Europe to take part in the Battle of Waterloo the following year. The Sixth Xhosa War of 1834–36, in South Africa, extended both his military and geographical experience and he returned there after his successes during the First Anglo-Sikh War. Several towns took either his name or that of his wife, most notably Ladysmith in KwaZulu-Natal. Known for his lightness of spirit and enthusiasm for his job, Smith was popular with his men and seemed to lead a charmed life on the battlefield, as well as enjoying a long and loving marriage off it. As one commentator put it, when reviewing Smith's rip-roaring autobiography, 'Harry Smith ranks among the happiest men that ever lived'.

Sir Hugh Wheeler (1789–1857), Brigadier-General. The son of an East India Company captain, Wheeler

As Governor General of India, Hardinge was Gough's superior in the political arena, but as an accomplished commander in his own right he also served as second-in-command on the battlefield. The dual roles would lead to controversy at the Battle of Ferozeshah. (Universal History Archive/Getty Images)

The architect of the 'battle without a mistake' (according to historian Sir John Fortescue), at Aliwal on 28 January 1846, Harry Smith was far from enamoured of the tactics of his commander-in-chief, Sir Hugh Gough. (Anne S.K. Brown Military Collection, Brown University Library)

reached India in 1805, at the age of 15, as a lieutenant in the 24th Native Infantry. He had made lieutenant-colonel by 1835 with the 48th Native Infantry, the regiment he served with in the First Anglo-Afghan War (1839–42). Wheeler commanded a brigade (including the 48th Native Infantry) during the First Anglo-Sikh War and again served with distinction in the Second Anglo-Sikh War (1848–49), being mentioned in despatches twice. His career continued its steady progression and he was made major-general in 1854, before being appointed commander of the Cawnpore Division in 1856. By now an old man, Wheeler's career and life came to a violent end during the Indian Mutiny of 1857. After surrendering to besieging forces at Cawnpore, Wheeler and most of his men were killed during the Satichaura Ghat massacre. Around 200 women and children suffered the same fate at the Bibighar massacre some days later.

Sir John Littler (1783–1856), Major-General. Cutting his teeth as an ensign in the 10th Bengal Native Infantry, Littler almost didn't make it to India, after his transport was captured by a French warship in the Bay of Bengal. Cut adrift in a pinnace, he and a number of other passengers made it to shore and he embarked upon a successful military career, rising to colonel of the 36th Bengal Native Infantry by 1839. A major-general two years later, he served as a divisional commander under Sir Hugh Gough at Maharajpore, on 29 December 1843, during the Gwalior Campaign. He was knighted the following year thanks to his conspicuous service, which had seen him wounded at the battle. He remained in India until 1851, when he returned to England with the rank of lieutenant-general.

SIKH

Lal Singh, Vizier and General (unknown–1866). The son of a shopkeeper, Lal Singh entered the Lahore Durbar as a lowly secretary. His father had been a favourite of Dhian Singh Dogra, while Lal Singh was favoured by Hira Singh, who made him treasurer and a raja in his own right. *Jagirs* (grants of land) at Rhotas, awarded by Hira Singh, and his installation as the tutor to the young Maharajah Dalip Singh, helped establish his position in the court, and he was willing to show a ruthless streak when opportunity arose. In 1843, he helped in the murder of one of his benefactors, Beli Ram, and he also turned on Hira Singh when it suited him.

A smooth-talking, charming individual, he became a favourite of Maharani Jindan and there were rumours that she had fallen pregnant by him. He certainly became one of her closest confidantes and was installed as a member of the Council of Regency. Promoted to *vizier* (the equivalent of prime minister) in November 1845, he had little aptitude for the job, nor was he an accomplished general, although he commanded a section of the Sikh Army during the First Anglo-Sikh War.

Although viewed with distrust on both sides, he was reinstated as *vizier* after the war, having briefly resigned his position, but was ousted again, this time by the British, when he attempted to interfere with the handing over of Kashmir to Gulab Singh.

Tej Singh (1799–1862), commander-in-chief. The nephew of Kushnal Singh, court chamberlain, Tej Singh hailed from Meerut and moved to Lahore to take advantage of his uncle's connections. Unlike Lal Singh, Tej Singh was a gifted soldier and rose quickly through the army, reaching the rank of general in 1818 at the age of just 19. Conspicuous service in Kashmir and Peshawar added to his reputation, and by the time he was 32, he was commanding 22 battalions in the Sikh Army. While campaigning alongside the British in the Khyber Pass in 1839, he met and became close to Nao Nihal Singh, the future maharajah, and Tej Singh became a key player in his rise to power at the expense of his father, Kharak Singh.

Tej Singh also showed an ability to switch sides at the right moment, turning his back on Nao Nihal's mother when the faction led by Dhian Singh Dogra gained the upper hand. Having switched sides in the nick of time, Tej remained in favour after Sher Singh's installation as maharajah. He was commander-in-chief at the outbreak of the war, but he engaged in correspondence with the British that revealed his animosity towards the army. This, and his subsequent actions on the battlefield, led to speculation that he had been turned by the British years earlier, possibly while campaigning in the Khyber Pass.

Gulab Singh (1792–1857), Raja of Jammu, Kashmir and Ladakh. Although he did not play an active part in the First Anglo-Sikh War, Gulab Singh's decision to keep his army out of the fighting was an important factor in the outcome of the conflict. He also epitomized the divisions within the Sikh Empire, being willing to trade a British victory for personal gain.

The province of Jammu had been conquered by the expansionist Ranjit Singh in 1808. Gulab Singh had fought against the invading forces but quickly recognized that further resistance was pointless against overwhelming odds. As a descendant of the rulers of Jammu, he was determined to win back what he saw as his birthright, but rather

Although his performance as a general during the war was abject, Lal Singh still enjoyed posing in full military garb when the opportunity arose. His treachery as one of the Sikh commanders doomed his army to defeat.

Tej Singh, commander-in-chief of the Sikh Army, was a noted and capable general, making treachery the only possible explanation for his total failure at the head of the powerful Sikh Army during the war. (Victoria and Albert Museum)

The owner of a powerful private army, Gulab Singh not only kept it out of the fighting during the First Anglo-Sikh War, he also plotted against the Sikh Army and helped to corrupt their supply chain.

than armed resistance he chose to ingratiate himself with the Lahore Durbar. Enlisting in Ranjit Singh's army, he served with such distinction (he even helped suppress the banditry of the rebel Mian Dedo in Jammu) that he was granted a *jagir* worth 40,000 rupees a year in 1820. By then, the Sikhs had also captured Kashmir, and in 1822 Gulab Singh was installed as Raja of Jammu and granted permission to raise and keep his own army. Alongside his two brothers, Suchet and Dhian, he formed the powerful 'Dogra brothers' faction that vied for control of the Sikh state.

Looking ahead to the death of Ranjit Singh and the inevitable turmoil that would follow, Gulab Singh determined to solidify his power base, invading Ladakh in 1834 and then moving further westwards to attack Tibet in 1841. Despite overreaching himself and suffering a serious defeat later that year, Gulab Singh's willingness to cooperate with the British was his trump card. It also helped that Britain had little interest in moving into the region of Jammu, Kashmir and Ladakh, as they bordered China rather than Russia. After keeping his army out of the war, he also acted as a negotiator during the subsequent peace talks, being granted Jammu and Kashmir (for the price of 7.5 million rupees) as recognition of his help. Gulab Singh's machinations had worked, as he was able to secure the independent Dogra state he had desired, and his descendants ruled Kashmir until 1947.

Ranjodh Singh Majithia (*c*.1821–72), General. Very little is known about this enigmatic character, who had an opportunity to change the course of the war when his 10,000-strong army crossed the Sutlej in January 1846 and stood unopposed with a variety of tempting targets to choose from. The son of one of Ranjit Singh's most trusted advisors, Ranjodh benefitted from a military education but seems to have had little aptitude for the profession. Family connections probably explain his rise to the rank of general in the Sikh Army. He was only around 25 years old when he faced Sir Harry Smith at Aliwal.

No hint of treachery has ever been associated with Ranjodh Singh but, cruelly for the Sikhs, in the one instance where they were led by a loyal general he happened to be incompetent. Accusations of cowardice have been levelled at him, and he certainly did little with his army after crossing the Sutlej near Ludhiana, but he was most probably simply an inept commander. Choosing to fight at Aliwal with the backs of his army against the river was a fatal mistake and helped the British to win a decisive victory. Following the war, he was involved in the negotiations that led to the Treaty of Lahore and was installed as one of the Council of Regency (to operate under the watch of a British resident) set up on 16 December 1846. Between the wars, he was involved in a long-running dispute with his brother, Lehna Singh, over hereditary rights (Lehna Singh claimed that Ranjodh Singh was actually the son of a slave girl and therefore not legitimate). In the build-up to the Second Anglo-Sikh War, Ranjodh Singh was suspected of conspiring against the British and was briefly imprisoned, although he was released when the war was over.

OPPOSING FORCES

BRITISH/BENGALI

In 1756, there were 150 men in the army of the Bengal Presidency. Under Robert Clive, that number built steadily until it reached more than 6,600 in 1763, and it passed 50,000 before the end of the century. Reforms to the organization and recruitment of the army of the East India Company continued to shape and reshape the forces at the command of the British as they increased their grip on the Subcontinent.

The major problem for the East India Company was recruitment. India was an unattractive destination for a would-be soldier. In fact, in the middle of the 18th century, many recruits would not even reach India, with large percentages dying en route. By the start of the 19th century, the death rate had fallen to 1.5 per cent, but getting to India was just part of the story. Climate and disease would then account for between 4.8 and 5.8 per cent of troops each year. Regiments usually stood at around half of their paper strength due to deaths and sickness.

Recruitment was also harder in times of war. During the Seven Years War, the American War of Independence, the French Revolutionary Wars

Regular British units were the cutting edge of the East India Company forces. The 16th Lancers are shown here in action against the disciplined infantry that formed the backbone of the Sikh Army after Ranjit Singh's reforms. (Anne S.K. Brown Military Collection, Brown University Library)

Gallerie der Costüme.

Officier,   Officierbursche,   Unterofficier.

Der Englisch-Ostindischen Armee 1843.

As well as relying on regular regiments sent over from Britain, the East India Company raised units locally. Whether composed of European or native troops, the officers were almost exclusively British. (Hulton Archive/Getty Images)

and the Napoleonic Wars, the number of men making the long journey from Britain to India slowed to a trickle. Those men that did reach India were often of a low quality in terms of size, health or intelligence. Lord Cornwallis, who took over as Governor General of India and commander-in-chief in 1786, wrote home the next year to comment on a batch of recruits recently arrived, stating, 'I did not think Britain could have furnished such a set of wretched objects ... For God's sake lose no time in taking up this business in a most serious manner.'

A crisis over recruitment reform saw the practice effectively grind to a halt at the end of the century, when just 85 men were sent to India between 1797 and January of 1799, but a solution was at hand. 'An Act for Better Recruiting of the Forces of the East India Company' was passed on 12 July 1799 and put the regular army in charge of recruitment for the East India Company, theoretically on an even standing. With war against France demanding manpower, however, the ratio of recruits was actually around 4:1 in favour of the British Army during the first five years following the passing of the act.

There were three main types of unit available to the British commanders at the outbreak of war with the Sikhs. First, and considered the most reliable of their troops, were regular British regiments. These were always in the minority, but were generally used as the cutting edge of the various ad hoc armies that were assembled throughout the period. As such, they also tended to suffer the highest casualty rates and were chronically short of men.

The second type were the European regiments raised in India. The 1st Bengal European Regiment was formed from a company that served with Clive at Plassey. Second European regiments were raised in all three presidencies (Bengal, Madras and Bombay) in 1824. Made up of a mixture of nationalities, these comprised a tiny portion of the East India Company forces.

Far more numerous were the native regiments. Originally employed as irregular forces, by the 1750s better training had helped mould them into more effective regular infantry. Now known as 'sepoys' (from the Persian word for an infantryman), the troops of the native regiments became gradually more experienced and effective. At the outbreak of the First Anglo-Sikh War, there were 74 battalions of sepoys in the army of the Bengal Presidency at the East India Company's disposal.

Cavalry was a mixture of light units and lancers, of which there were a combined eight regiments. Joining them was the Governor General's Bodyguard, a unit made up of the cream of the other regiments, and there were also 18 regiments of irregular horsemen. Artillery was comprised of three brigades of horse artillery (each with three European and one native troop), five battalions of European Foot Artillery and two Native Foot Artillery battalions.

Commanders in India therefore had a difficult balancing act to perform. They could not rely totally on their British regiments because there simply weren't enough of them. The sepoy regiments were, whether fairly or not, considered inferior, yet they would necessarily make up the bulk of any army.

The Army of the Sutlej, scrambled together to take on the Sikhs, was no exception. Brigades were usually formed with a core British or European regiment supplemented by one or two native units. Brigades that were assigned less important areas of a battlefield might be comprised solely of native units, and native regiments would usually draw service as garrison troops and baggage-train guards when they were required. Nevertheless, despite the habitual downgrading of their performance by their commanding officers, who looked to their British units when handing out laurels after a victory, the sepoy regiments were capable of performing well in battle.

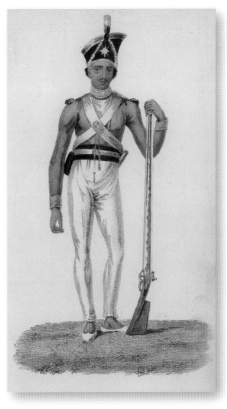

Native soldiers, known as 'sepoys' formed the majority of regiments available to the East India Company. Though generally reckoned by British officers to be inferior to their European or British counterparts, they were capable of performing at a high level. (Florilegius/SSPL/Getty Images)

Lord Cornwallis, though best remembered for surrendering at Yorktown during the American War of Independence, helped reform the organization of the East India Company's armed forces at the end of the 18th century. (Anne S.K. Brown Military Collection, Brown University Library)

The second major issue for Sir Hugh Gough on the outbreak of war was the dispersed nature of British troops in the region. If he had been able to gather all of the units within a reasonable range, he could have fielded an army of around 35,000, which would have been ample for facing down the threat of the Sikh Army. In reality, he could amass far fewer men, especially in the early days of the conflict when troops were marching from various bases to join him. Even at the final engagement of the war, at Sobraon, he only fielded around 20,000, with garrisons and other detached commands leeching men away. Gough's impetuous style and unwillingness to wait for reinforcements allowed the Sikhs to enter most of the actions of the war with equal or superior numbers. Even with the ruinous nature of the Sikh command structure, and the outright treachery of its two main generals, this almost proved Gough's undoing.

Although infantry modelled on European lines had become the core of the Sikh Army by the time they came to fight the British, irregular units still had a role to play. (Anne S.K. Brown Military Collection, Brown University Library)

European officers like the Italian Paolo Avitabile helped train the soldiers of Ranjit Singh's new army. Although Avitabile had left the Sikh service by the time of the war, the brigade he had commanded continued to be viewed as an elite unit.

SIKH

The Sikh Army was totally transformed under the rule of Ranjit Singh, starting around 1805 and continuing after his death in 1839. The traditional model of massed cavalry forces dominating the army was considered outdated, and a new system, built primarily on disciplined infantry backed up by a powerful artillery arm, became the standard.

The problem was, few were interested in enlisting in these unpopular services and the job of transforming the army took decades. The process may have been slow, but it was also highly effective: by the time the Sikhs went to war in 1845, they arguably possessed the most powerful army ever faced by the British in India, but the political fallout following the death of Ranjit Singh had already started to undermine its effectiveness.

The first battalion of infantry trained along European lines made its appearance in 1805. This became the foundation stone of the *Faij-i-quawa'idan* (drilled force), more commonly called the *Fauj-i-ain* (regular army). Initially limited to infantry battalions, this new regular army came to include cavalry and artillery as well, but in strictly supporting roles.

There were nine battalions of infantry by 1812, and in the 1820s the introduction of foreign advisors added extra discipline and know-how. The regular army gradually became a more attractive proposition as the quality of the infantry improved. The pay was tempting and, more importantly, reliable – even if it was often delayed for months, it would eventually be delivered. By 1831, there were 21 battalions of infantry and a decade later there were 31, totalling 27,000 men.

This rapid expansion of the army, and uncertainty over its extent, generated tension as the British struggled to get a grasp on this potential threat and frequently overestimated the number of men under arms in the Sikh Army. European officers, including notable names like the Italian Paolo Avitabile and the Frenchman Claude Auguste Court, put their stamp on the new regiments, and by the end of Ranjit Singh's reign there were an estimated 50 Europeans imparting their wisdom to the growing army. That all changed in the instability following Ranjit Singh's death. As the soldiers became hostile to their officers in general, and to the Europeans in particular, several were killed by their men and most of the rest saw that it was time to look elsewhere for employment. Only three European officers are known to have served with the Sikhs during the war, and there were a few deserters dotted among the ranks as well.

In 1822, Ranjit Singh had switched from modelling his army on the British military system to that of the French, and this process had mostly been completed by the time of his death. With this transformation came the formation of the first brigade in the army. Initially infantry only, this was expanded to eventually include cavalry and artillery and was known as the French Legion, although it was more officially called the *Fauj-i-khas* ('royal army'). At the outbreak of the First Anglo-Sikh War, the brigade had 3,176 infantrymen, 1,667 cavalry and 34 guns. Other brigades were formed on the same model, notably that of Avitabile (known as 'Avitabile's Brigade' or simply 'the Avitabiles'), which bore his name even after he left the Sikh service in 1843. Total *Fauj-i-ain* numbers increased to more than 35,000 by

A Sikh shield, dating from approximately 1830. The gold-overlay decoration depicts Ranjit Singh, the 'Lion of Lahore'. (Universal Images Group/Getty Images)

1838 and to an unmanageable 70,000 by 1845. Just before the outbreak of war, in 1844, a further modification had been made, with the formation of seven divisions within the army.

Sikh cavalry may have fallen from its elite status, but the cavalry arm of the main army, numbering around 6,235 in 1845, was a fairly disciplined force. By 1838, it comprised two lancer regiments and six dragoon regiments, while two regiments of cuirassiers were added a year later. Less disciplined, because they received no training whatsoever, were the 22,000 or so irregular cavalrymen known as the *Fauj-i-sowari*, or 'cavalry army'. More commonly called *ghorchurras*, they could not be relied upon to stand up to an organized enemy, but could harass and pursue a broken foe. Service in this force was much more attractive to the average Sikh horseman, as it had the weight of tradition behind it and did not demand unpalatable things like training and discipline.

The artillery arm was also steadily built up under Ranjit Singh. He scraped together guns wherever he could and set up his own foundries, but standardization was not a priority. Of the 252 guns captured by the British during the First Anglo-Sikh War, there were an astonishing 96 different calibres. From 40 guns in 1808, to 192 at the time of Ranjit Singh's death, the Sikh artillery arm had expanded to 381 by 1845, and there were also 388 swivel guns. British preconceptions led them to consider the Sikh artillery to be inferior to their own at the outbreak of the war, but they were swiftly disabused of that notion once hostilities opened.

Secondary to the *Fauj-i-ain* was the feudal army, the *Jagirdari Fauj*. Provided by Sikh nobles (depending on the noble's estate, he would have to provide more or less men), the quota was usually made up of irregular cavalry, but came to include infantry and artillery as well. As many as 55,000 of these troops were available at the start of the war. Gulab Singh in particular was notable for having 10,000–15,000 infantry at his disposal, along with nearly 2,000 cavalry and 94 guns. Garrison troops, meanwhile, were simply stationed at forts throughout the empire. Sometimes backed up by regular troops, they were never called to serve in the field.

One final group to consider in the Sikh Army is the *Akalis*, or *Nihangs*. Religious zealots, they had been unruly even before the breakdown of authority within the army. They could be counted on to fight bravely, even recklessly, but they could not be counted on to take orders. The troublesome *Akalis* had actually suffered the same fate as was now planned for the entire Sikh Army, as Ranjit Singh had deliberately whittled down their numbers in battle. A thousand or so took part in the First Anglo-Sikh War, fighting as mounted infantry.

Akalis were religious fanatics who were as much a menace to the local population as to enemy units. Fighting as mounted infantry, and foraging freely upon the land, they were considered more trouble than they were worth and had been steadily eroded under Ranjit Singh's leadership. The First Anglo-Sikh War was their last hurrah. (Anne S.K. Brown Military Collection, Brown University Library)

ORDERS OF BATTLE

BATTLE OF MUDKI, 18 DECEMBER 1845

BRITISH/BENGALI (ARMY OF THE SUTLEJ)

Lieutenant-General Sir Hugh Gough
12,350 men and 42 guns
1st Division (Major-General Sir Harry Smith)
HM 31st Foot, 24th and 47th Native Infantry (Brigadier Bolton)
HM 50th Foot, 42nd and 48th Native Infantry (Brigadier Wheeler)
2nd Division (Major-General Walter Gilbert)
2nd and 16th Native Grenadiers and 45th Native Infantry
3rd Division (Major-General Sir John McCaskill)
HM 9th and 80th Foot, 26th and 73rd Native Infantry
  (Brigadier Wallace)
Cavalry Division
3rd Light Dragoons, 4th Native Light Cavalry (one wing)
  (Brigadier White)
5th Native Light Cavalry, Governor General's Bodyguard
  (Brigadier Gough)
9th Native Irregular Horse, 4th Native Light Cavalry (one wing)
  (Brigadier Mactier)
Artillery (Lieutenant-Colonel Brooke, acting brigadier)
Five troops of horse artillery and two light field batteries

SIKH

General Lal Singh
Infantry
Between 2,000 and 3,000
Cavalry
Between 1,500 and 12,000 regular and irregular cavalry
Artillery
18 guns, four howitzers

BATTLE OF FEROZESHAH, 21–22 DECEMBER 1845

BRITISH/BENGALI (ARMY OF THE SUTLEJ)

Lieutenant-General Sir Hugh Gough
18,000 men and 69 guns
1st Division (Major-General Sir Harry Smith)
42nd and 48th Native Infantry, HM 50th Foot (Brigadier Ryan)
47th and 24th Native Infantry, HM 31st Foot (Brigadier Hicks)
2nd Division (Major-General Walter Gilbert)
16th Native Grenadiers, 45th Native Infantry, 1st European Light
  Infantry (Brigadier McLaran)
41st Native Infantry, HM 80th and 29th Foot (Brigadier Taylor)
3rd Division (Lieutenant-General Sir Henry Hardinge)
HM 9th Foot and 26th Native Infantry (Colonel Wallace)
2nd Native Grenadiers, 73rd Native Infantry (Colonel McLaren)
4th Division (Major-General Sir John Littler)
54th, 33rd and 44th Native Infantry (Brigadier Ashburnham)
14th and 12th Native Infantry, HM 62nd Foot (Brigadier Reed)
Cavalry Division
3rd Native Irregular Cavalry and 8th Native Light Cavalry
  (Lieutenant-Colonel Harriett)
5th Native Light Cavalry and Governor General's Bodyguard
  (Brigadier Gough)
4th Native Light Cavalry, 3rd Light Dragoons (Lieutenant-Colonel
  White)
Artillery (Lieutenant-Colonel Brooke, acting brigadier)
Six troops of horse artillery, four batteries of 9-pdrs, one troop of
  howitzers

SIKH

General Lal Singh
Infantry
Approximately 7,000 regular infantry, including Avitabile's Brigade
Cavalry
Approximately 8,000 regular cavalry
Irregulars
Approximately 7,000 irregular infantry and cavalry
Artillery
103 guns

BATTLE OF ALIWAL, 28 JANUARY 1846

BRITISH/BENGALI

Major-General Sir Harry Smith
10,000 men and 32 guns
1st Division (Major-General Sir Harry Smith)
Nusseree Battalion of Gurkhas and 36th Native Infantry
  (Brigadier Godby)
HM 31st Foot, 24th and 47th Native Infantry (Brigadier Hicks)
2nd Division (Major-General Walter Gilbert)
HM 50th Foot, 48th Native Infantry, Sirmoor Battalion of Gurkhas
  (Brigadier Wheeler)
HM 53rd Foot, 30th Native Infantry and Shekhawatee Brigade
  infantry (Brigadier Wilson)
Cavalry Division (Brigadier Charles Robert Cureton)
16th Lancers and 3rd Native Light Cavalry (Brigadier MacDowell)
1st and 5th Native Light Cavalry, Governor General's Bodyguard,
  4th Native Irregular Cavalry and Shekhawatee Brigade cavalry
  (Brigadier Stedman)
Artillery (Major Lawrenson)
30 guns, plus two 8in. howitzers

SIKH

General Ranjodh Singh
Infantry
Approximately 4,000 regular infantry, including Avitabile's Brigade,
  and approximately 8,000 irregular infantry
Cavalry
Approximately 2,000 irregular cavalry
Artillery
52 guns

BATTLE OF SOBRAON, 10 FEBRUARY 1846

BRITISH/BENGALI (ARMY OF THE SUTLEJ)

Lieutenant-General Sir Hugh Gough
20,000 men and 108 guns
1st Division (Major-General Sir Harry Smith)
HM 31st Foot, 24th and 47th Native Infantry, Nusseree Battalion of
  Gurkhas (Brigadier Penny)
HM 50th Foot, 42nd Native Infantry (Brigadier Hicks)
2nd Division (Major-General Walter Gilbert)
1st European Light Infantry, 16th Native Infantry and Sirmoor
  Battalion of Gurkhas (Brigadier McLaran)
HM 29th Foot, 41st and 68th Native Infantry (Brigadier Taylor)
3rd Division (Major-General Sir Robert Dick)
HM 10th and 53rd Foot, 43rd and 59th Native Infantry (Brigadier Stacey)

HM 80th Foot and 33rd Native Infantry (Brigadier Wilkinson)
Reserve (Brigadier Ashburnham)
HM 9th Foot and 26th Native Infantry
4th and 5th Native Infantry
Cavalry Division (Major-General Sir Joseph Thackwell)
3rd Light Dragoons, 3rd and 9th Native Irregular Cavalry
    (Brigadier Scott)
16th Lancers, 3rd, 4th and 5th Native Light Cavalry (Brigadier Charles
    Robert Cureton)
9th Lancers (Brigadier Campbell)
Artillery Division (Brigadier Gowan)
108 guns, including six 18-pdrs, three 12-pdrs (rebored 9-pdrs), five
    24-lb howitzers, six 8in. howitzers and six 5.5in. howitzers

SIKH

General Tej Singh
Infantry
Approximately 20,000 infantry, with both regular (including
    Avitabile's Brigade) and irregular units present
Cavalry
Approximately 1,000 irregular cavalry
Artillery
67 guns and 200 *jingalls*

The Sikhs' artillery strength grew steadily throughout Ranjit Singh's reign, with myriad calibres taking their place in a formidable force. The Zamzama Great Gun, shown here, was a symbol of Sikh military prowess, although it did not take part in the war. (Vincent Clarence Scott O'Connor/Royal Geographical Society/Getty Images)

OPPOSING PLANS

BRITISH

The British had amassed a wealth of experience in fighting native armies on the Indian Subcontinent. The *Khalsa* would undoubtedly provide the sternest challenge they had yet faced, but they had encountered armies with strong European influences before. In particular, fighting in the Anglo-Mysore and Anglo-Maratha wars had pitched British and native units against disciplined forces that had absorbed lessons from the European style of warfare.

Against Hyder Ali and then his son, Tipu Sultan, the British fought four wars between 1767 and 1799. Hyder Ali was on good terms with the French and employed several officers, as well as a number of French mercenary units. However, his army retained its cavalry bias and he was not interested in a European-style infantry arm (French expertise was welcomed in the scientific field of artillery). At the start of the Second Anglo-Mysore War (1780–84), he invaded British territory with a huge army of 80,000 men, the majority of them cavalry. The imaginative use of his forces during the first two Anglo-Mysore wars allowed Hyder Ali to frustrate British infantry and even score stunning victories, but the British learned their lesson quickly. During the Third

The British had confronted numerous threats to their dominance in the region and repeatedly showed an ability to adapt to new challenges. Here, they face Mysore forces at the Siege of Cuddalore in 1783. (Anne S.K. Brown Military Collection, Brown University Library)

Maratha light cavalry made a decisive contribution to the Third Anglo-Mysore War for the British, countering the cavalry of Tipu Sultan. (Anne S.K. Brown Military Collection, Brown University Library)

The Battle of Assaye, reckoned by the Duke of Wellington to be his finest ever victory, saw the British cripple the Maratha Army by buying off a large portion of its officer corps.

Anglo-Mysore War (1790–92), Lord Cornwallis employed cavalry of his own, a 12,000-strong force of Maratha light cavalry, which was able to keep Tipu Sultan's horsemen at bay while infantry and artillery laid siege to Seringapatam. The British had shown a willingness and ability to adapt to the warfare being waged against them, but their next formative experience involved an enemy that was more interested in copying European tactics.

The Maratha leader Mahadji Sindhia in many ways anticipated the rule of Ranjit Singh in the Punjab. Like the great Sikh leader, Sindhia recognized the growing power of the East India Company and built an army to confront it. Following the British style of training, rather than the French, Sindhia came to rely on a 2,000-strong unit led by a European officer, Benoît de Boigne, which had expanded to 27,000 by the end of the 18th century. As with the Sikhs on the death of Ranjit Singh, matters deteriorated for the Marathas following the death of Sindhia in 1794. The British, uncertain of tackling such a strong army head-on, engaged in subterfuge, once more showing their ability to adapt to circumstances. With most of the junior and mid-level officers in the Maratha Army being British or of Anglo-Indian heritage, they were vulnerable to bribery and the British bought many of them off, leaving a hole in the army's command structure which its inept leadership then widened by removing the remainder of the British officers, suspecting their loyalty. When Arthur Wellesley confronted the Marathas at Assaye, he faced and defeated a fatally crippled opponent.

Against the Sikhs, the British had no need to undermine the enemy's command structure: the Sikhs had done a perfectly good job of that themselves. The systematic removal of the experienced officers and their replacement by the politically adept had been followed by a breakdown in both discipline and training. The Sikh Army was therefore a shadow of its former self at the outbreak of the war and the main concern for the British was its size – even a declining army could inflict a defeat if it had overwhelming numbers. The primary goal of the British, therefore, was to prevent the linking up of the three smaller armies under Tej Singh, Lal Singh and Ranjodh Singh (the self-interest of Gulab Singh kept his men out of the picture). The cooperation of the Sikh generals with the British cause (Ranjodh Singh excepted) could also not be relied upon long term, as the troops of their armies might at any moment tire of their inept leadership and install commanders loyal to the Sikh cause, with potentially disastrous results.

The haste with which Sir Hugh Gough moved therefore makes more sense when viewed in the context of the campaign. Tackling the individual Sikh corps quickly, even if that meant going into battle with equally matched or slightly inferior forces, was the safest route to victory.

SIKH

The actual plans of the Sikh Army are harder to ascertain, given the treachery of its leadership. There is reason to believe that the ruling class saw the war as a win-win scenario. If the army was smashed, then its reign of terror would be at an end. If it defeated the British, then the Sikh Empire could expand into new territories, bringing more wealth into the state and allowing it to keep the soldiers happy with regular payment of wages, thus defusing the danger they posed to the ruling elite. After all, the continued expansion of the army after the Sikh Empire had run out of room itself was one of the primary causes of the breakdown in discipline.

Even shorn of effective generalship, the Sikh soldiers, especially their artillery crews, were brave and stubborn. They had no thought but to defeat their opponents on the battlefield, tragically leaving concepts such as tactics and strategy to their commanders. Battlefield tactics relied almost exclusively on adopting and attempting to hold defensive positions. Even where the Sikhs gained the upper hand, such as at the end of the first day's fighting at Ferozeshah and during Sir Harry Smith's march past Bhudowal, they held back from switching to an offensive that might have resulted in victories. Most notable in this regard was the inactivity of the cavalry corps, which was little more than a spectator at most of the engagements and missed numerous opportunities to tip the balance.

The common Sikh soldiers deserved much better, but it cannot be denied that, as the plan of their commanders was to weaken or cripple their own army, that plan was carried forth to great effect.

Ranjit Singh had been able to keep his vast army under control, and to keep its wages flowing, but the situation changed dramatically upon his death. (Universal History Archive/Getty Images)

THE CAMPAIGN

Opinion is divided on the exact day that Sikh forces crossed the Sutlej, with dates suggested between 8 and 15 December, although 11 December is generally accepted as the most likely. What is certain is that this was not technically an invasion. The Sikhs merely occupied Sikh territory south of the river, although it obviously stretched the terms of the 1809 Treaty of Amritsar, which had recognized British control over the region. Nevertheless, the move offered enough of a pretext for the British to claim Sikh aggressiveness had made war unavoidable. Britain had already broken off diplomatic relations with Lahore on 3 December, now the Sikhs had crossed the Sutlej, 'without a shadow of provocation,' according to Hardinge. It was a flimsy excuse for war, and Hardinge privately had doubts about how things would be viewed back home, especially considering the help offered by the Sikhs in Afghanistan.

With Lal Singh and Tej Singh in command of the two Sikh corps to venture over the river (Lal Singh's men crossing at Harike, Tej Sing at Attaree, closer to Ferozepore), the position was uncertain. Neither men were Sikh, and although Tej Singh was a respected general, he was also sympathetic to the

The town of Ferozepore, including its fort, was garrisoned by a substantial force of around 7,000 men, but was extremely vulnerable to the far superior Sikh numbers that crossed the Sutlej on 11 December. (Universal History Archive/UIG via Getty Images)

British troop dispersal, December 1845

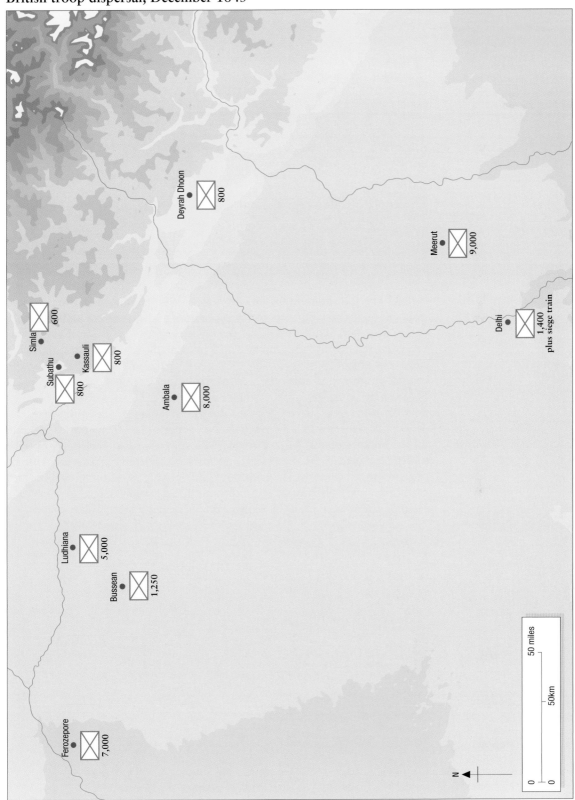

Deyrah Dhoon 800

Meerut 9,000

Simla 600

Subathu 800

Kassauli 800

Ambala 8,000

Delhi 1,400 plus siege train

Ludhiana 5,000

Bussean 1,250

Ferozepore 7,000

N

0
0

50km
50 miles

A Sikh army on the move, with its sizeable artillery train handled by elephants. The massive superiority in artillery enjoyed by the Sikhs at the beginning of the war would be steadily eroded as British forces captured guns at each battle. (Universal History Archive/UIG via Getty Images)

British. The situation within the army itself was also unsettled: officers were being made to carry muskets by their men, which was seen as humiliating. As many as 43,000 Sikhs crossed the river, with around 23,000 of that number being disciplined infantry, along with a large artillery contingent numbering some 150 guns.

Lal Singh based the main army, totalling around 25,000 men, at Ferozeshah, while Tej Singh, commanding around 18,500 men, entered into a half-hearted siege of Ferozepore. The British situation was still potentially desperate, with a small garrison at Ferozepore (7,000 men and 12 guns under Major-General John Littler), even fewer men at Ludhiana (5,000, under Brigadier H. M. Wheeler), and further scattered garrisons serving to dissipate their strength. The Sikh forces had an opportunity to combine and eradicate each British position in turn, and there was no need to hurry. Sir Hugh Gough, with 10,000 men, was on his way but still 250km distant.

The foothills of the Himalayas were the base for two Gurkha units, the Nusseree and Sirmoor battalions, both of whom performed with distinction after trekking to join the British forces engaging the Sikh Army. (Print Collector/Getty Images)

Opening moves, 12–18 December 1845

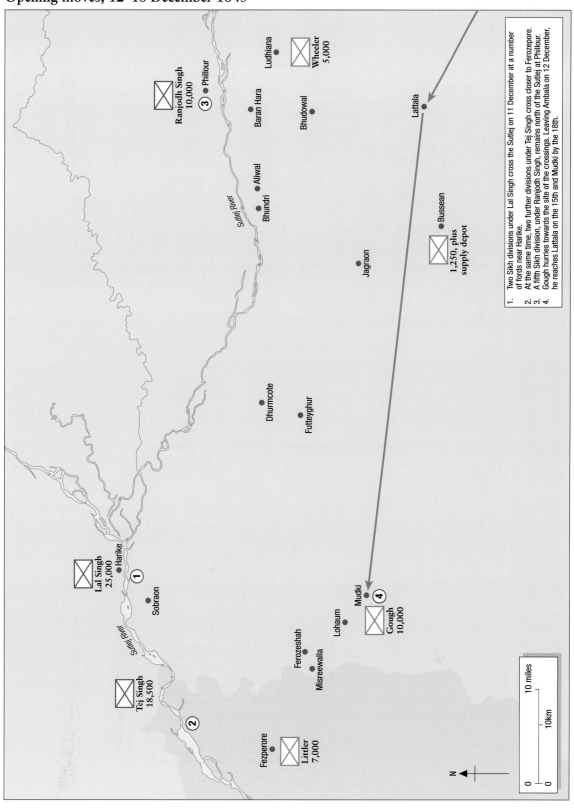

Ludhiana

Wheeler
5,000

Ranjodh Singh
10,000

③ ● Phillour

Baran Hara

Bhudowal

Lattala

Sutlej River

Aliwal

Bhundri

Bussean

1,250, plus
supply depot

Jagraon

Dhurmcote

Futteyghur

Harike

Lal Singh
25,000

①

Sobraon

Mudki

④

Gough
10,000

Lohaum

Sutlej River

Tej Singh
18,500

②

Ferozeshah

Misreewalla

Fezperore

Littler
7,000

1. Two Sikh divisions under Lal Singh cross the Sutlej on 11 December at a number of fords near Harike.
2. At the same time, two further divisions under Tej Singh cross closer to Ferozepore.
3. A fifth Sikh division, under Ranjodh Singh, remains north of the Sutlej at Phillour.
4. Gough hurries towards the site of the crossings. Leaving Ambala on 12 December, he reaches Lattala on the 15th and Mudki by the 18th.

N

0 ———— 10 miles
0 ———— 10km

Sir Charles Napier, who had controversially annexed the Sind in 1843, was on the march with a 15,000-strong army, but Gough was not prepared to await his arrival before acting. (Anne S.K. Brown Military Collection, Brown University Library)

The situation was indeed dangerous, but less desperate than it appeared. Upon crossing the Sutlej, Tej Singh had sent word to Ferozepore, professing his affection for the British and asking for instructions. Captain Peter Nicholson, the assistant political agent at Ferozepore, had responded, asking Tej Singh to refrain from attacking the town and to hold the *Khalsa* back as long as possible. 'Halt as many days as you can,' Nicholson wrote, 'and then march towards the Governor General.' If Tej Singh was able to carry this off, the British would have time to combine their forces.

Curiously, Littler appears to have been kept out of the loop regarding this neat little agreement: the British commander at Ferozepore made repeated attempts to engage the Sikhs besieging the town. Tej Singh was able to pull his men back each time, but such a dynamic situation could easily have exploded into violence, with potentially dire consequences for the British. The Sikh soldiers were understandably irked at being denied the opportunity to attack the defiant British, and puzzled as to why the town was not being properly invested: the south had been left open, allowing either a retreat by Littler or the approach of reinforcements.

Gough, meanwhile, was accelerating towards his link-up with the forces facing the Sikhs, the rapidness of his reaction to the declaration of war bearing testimony to the extent of British preparations. On 12 December, his men covered 25km (16 miles). The following day they marched 29km, then 32, 48 and 48 on subsequent days. On 16 December, he reached Bussean (site of a major supply depot), meeting the Governor General and troops from Ludhiana and leaving his heavy baggage there, before moving on towards Wudnee. As he approached Ferozepore, however, it became clear that the Sikh commanders were sticking to their side of the bargain and not pressing matters. Gough took the opportunity to slow the pace of his march (only 16km were covered on 17 December), giving his men time to recover, if only a little, from their exertions.

If the campaign could be spun out, there was the prospect of further reinforcements. There were 9,000 men at Meerut, a pair of Gurkha regiments based at Simla and Dehra Dun and regiments at both Kassauli and Subathu. A British regiment (the 53rd Foot) and the Shekhawatee Brigade were also within reasonable distance, and, in the longer term, around 15,000 men under Sir Charles Napier could be brought up from Sind. But Gough was not of a mind to take things too slowly. On 18 December, he continued his advance towards the Sikh forces, heading towards Mudki.

THE BATTLE OF MUDKI

Lal Singh, with an army at Ferozeshah greatly outnumbering Gough's, now detached a small force, variously estimated at between 3,000 and 15,000 men (the latter number would no doubt have included thousands of irregular cavalry), to confront the marching British. The detachment was too small to seriously hamper Gough's progress, and there were murmurings among the Sikh soldiery about the decision.

A number of Sikhs occupied Mudki itself, including the village's small fort, but the bulk of the detached force lined up in front of the village of Lohaum. It was mid-afternoon before the British began to arrive, and the advanced Sikh units quickly fell back to alert the men at Lohaum. It had been a hard march for the British, in blistering heat, and Gough himself admitted that his men were 'in a state of great exhaustion'. As each unit arrived at the village, they made straight for the small lake to satisfy their raging thirst. Dust had made the march miserable, and a cloud of it away towards Lohaum betrayed the position of the Sikh detachment, making it clear that a significant body of men was within striking distance. Despite the lateness of the hour and the fatigue of his men, Gough decided to attack at once.

Mudki was a sizeable village of around 4,000 inhabitants. To the west was cultivated land to a range of around 4km. After this, a belt of jungle a kilometre wide, as well as an area of sandy hills, prevented any clear view of Lohaum. The jungle was an obstruction for both sides, but it was the British who were advancing and it was they who would need to find a way through to reach the Sikh lines, positioned on its opposite edge.

The Sikhs took up a defensive position, with between 2,000 and 3,000 infantry supported by 22 guns. On each flank of this line was a body of cavalry, made up of both regular and irregular units, with estimates of their combined strength ranging as high as 12,000. The British were advancing in greater strength (especially considering the unreliability of the Sikh

The 3rd Light Dragoons were part of the cavalry action that cleared the Sikh horsemen from the field, but they suffered heavy losses while advancing through jungle to tackle the Sikh artillery.

Battle of Mudki, 18 December 1845

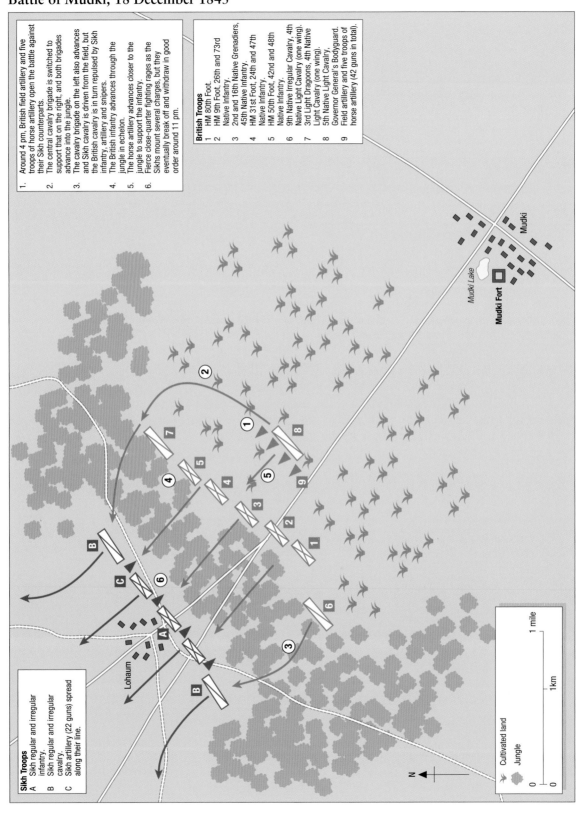

Sikh Troops

A Sikh regular and irregular infantry.
B Sikh regular and irregular cavalry.
C Sikh artillery (22 guns) spread along their line.

British Troops

1 HM 80th Foot.
2 HM 9th Foot, 26th and 73rd Native Infantry.
3 2nd and 16th Native Grenadiers, 45th Native Infantry.
4 HM 31st Foot, 24th and 47th Native Infantry.
5 HM 50th Foot, 42nd and 48th Native Infantry.
6 9th Native Irregular Cavalry, 4th Native Light Cavalry (one wing).
7 3rd Light Dragoons, 4th Native Light Cavalry (one wing).
8 5th Native Light Cavalry.
9 Governor General's Bodyguard. Field artillery and five troops of horse artillery (42 guns in total).

1. Around 4 pm, British field artillery and five troops of horse artillery open the battle against their Sikh counterparts.
2. The central cavalry brigade is switched to support that on the right, and both brigades advance into the jungle.
3. The cavalry brigade on the left also advances and Sikh cavalry is driven from the field, but the British cavalry is in turn repulsed by Sikh infantry, artillery and snipers.
4. The British infantry advances through the jungle in echelon.
5. The horse artillery advances closer to the jungle to support the infantry.
6. Fierce close-quarter fighting rages as the Sikhs mount several charges, but they eventually break off and withdraw in good order around 11 pm.

Cultivated land

Jungle

0   1km

0   1 mile

N

Mudki

Mudki Lake

Mudki Fort

Lohaum

ghorchurras), with close to 4,000 European infantry, 8,500 sepoys and 42 guns. The British lined up with the 1st Division, under Sir Harry Smith, on the right, the 2nd Division, under Walter Raleigh Gilbert, in the centre and the 3rd Division, under Sir John McCaskill, on the left. The right wing of the army was by far the stronger and would lead the advance, with the other divisions following in echelon. Three cavalry brigades were deployed, initially positioned on the left, centre and right of the British artillery.

It is unclear if Gough intended to open the battle with an artillery duel, or if they were simply the first of his units to be in position to attack, but this was how the action commenced, around 4 p.m. (Gough suggested in his report on the battle that he was concerned the Sikhs were advancing to take possession of the plain beyond the jungle and wanted to contest any such move, so he called up his cavalry and artillery as the quickest possible response. The Sikhs were actually awaiting a British advance.) Despite a significant advantage in numbers, however, the British gunners were unable to achieve dominance over their Sikh opponents (initial shots were exploratory as visibility was so poor, but gun crews were then able to aim at the muzzle flashes of their opponents). After an hour of ineffectual fire, Gough sent his cavalry in. There was a dual purpose in this: the cavalry would hopefully silence the Sikh guns, but would also prevent the cavalry massed on each wing of the Sikh line from overlapping the British infantry, which was forming up in a second line behind the artillery.

The cavalry that was initially deployed in the centre of the British formation (comprising the 5th Native Light Cavalry and the Governor General's Bodyguard) was shifted to reinforce the right immediately prior to the attack. Although outnumbered, superior discipline told and the Sikh cavalry (mainly irregular *ghorchurras*) was quickly driven from the field. However, in advancing into the jungle the British horsemen became disorganized and many fell victim to Sikh snipers operating from the cover offered by the trees and bushes. What should have been a decisive advantage, with British cavalry getting behind the Sikh line and spreading chaos, therefore melted away as the British suffered what Sir Harry Smith termed 'a very considerable and most unnecessary loss'. The British cavalry was in turn forced to withdraw, and the field was left to the infantry to decide the outcome.

What was now a clear superiority in numbers in favour of the British meant this outcome was never in doubt, but the Sikhs offered stiff resistance. They had to manage without a commander, however, as Lal Singh had fled the battlefield along with his cavalry. The three British infantry divisions now advanced in echelon, with Sir Harry Smith's 1st Division, on the right, leading the way. This, the strongest division on the battlefield, was made up of two British regiments, HM 31st and 50th Foot, along with the 24th, 42nd, 47th and 48th Native Infantry. This was intended to be the driving force in the British assault and, inevitably, saw the hardest fighting and took the heaviest casualties.

The centre of the line was comprised entirely of sepoys, and only three regiments of them (the 2nd, 16th Native Grenadiers and the 45th Native Infantry), while the left saw HM 9th and 80th Foot advance alongside the 26th and 73rd Native Infantry.

A rumour of the return of Sikh cavalry temporarily forced the 50th Foot to form square on the right, and similar precautions were taken on the opposite flank before it became clear that there was no such threat and the advance continued. The snipers that had plagued the British cavalry now tackled Smith's men as they struggled through the thorn bushes and trees. As men fell, order was lost. 'Immediately the regiment was entirely broken up in utter confusion,' commented Colonel James Robertson of the 31st Foot. Other observers claimed that the sepoy units in the 1st Division fell behind the advance of the two British regiments and that subsequently friendly fire was a problem in the confusion, made worse by the dust and the failing light. Some witnesses went so far as to claim that as many as half the casualties suffered by the British were inflicted by their own comrades.

When the two lines finally came face to face, fierce close-quarter fighting erupted as the Sikhs refused to give ground. A confused mêlée ensued, with no chance for officers to exert any influence on their scattered men. Sir Harry Smith's recollection of the battle was confused in the extreme. He mentioned that the dust was so severe that all vision was obscured and he seems to have had little grasp of the Sikh positions or movements during the chaotic affair. The endless low rumble of Sikh kettle drums provided an eerie soundtrack to the fighting, which continued for hours. Some reports suggest there were a number of charges by the Sikhs, perhaps as many as three, though how committed these were, or how many troops were involved, would have been impossible to ascertain under the circumstances. Around 9 p.m. the Sikhs began to give ground, pulling back towards Lohaum, and the British were able to capture most of their guns, although stubborn Sikh resistance would see some of the guns change hands several times. Around 11 p.m. the Sikhs finally began to withdraw completely, retaining good order as

The 31st Regiment, from Sir Harry Smith's division, advance against the Sikh line at Mudki. The regiment fought in all the major engagements of the war. (Anne S.K. Brown Military Collection, Brown University Library)

they disengaged. Sporadic fighting would continue for another hour, and some British bodies were found far to the west of Lohaum, indicating a very determined pursuit of the withdrawing Sikhs, as well as continuing resistance. Around midnight, peace finally descended over the battlefield. As the dust settled, the victorious British became aware that a bright moon had risen. The small Sikh force fell back towards Ferozeshah, while the exhausted British troops dragged themselves back to Mudki, at times sniped at by Sikh riflemen still hidden in the jungle.

Casualties are believed to have been fairly even, although British reports exaggerated both the size of the Sikh force engaged, and its losses. The 1st Division bore the brunt of the fighting and suffered total losses of 437, which included 79 killed and 339 wounded. The cavalry also suffered badly, with the 3rd Light Dragoons taking 101 casualties out of 497 men engaged. Total losses across the army numbered 215 dead and 657 wounded. Eyewitnesses estimated equal losses for the Sikhs, and it was noted that many of their wounded refused help and preferred to die quietly on the battlefield than receive treatment.

The night following the battle was grim, with plummeting temperatures adding to the woes of the British troops, who had marched for half of the preceding day and then fought for the remainder of it. There was an awareness that they had met a formidable and dangerous enemy, and although there was satisfaction over a hard-fought victory, there was also the realization that the war was not going to be easy. There are also indications that the British officers had underestimated their opponents, perhaps used to native armies crumbling under the disciplined assaults of the East India Company's forces. One British infantryman remembered, 'I heard several officers say, "O, they will run away before we get up to them—they will not fight us."' If such sentiments had been widespread before Mudki, they must have been swiftly reconsidered.

Of the 22 Sikh guns engaged at Mudki, the British had captured 15, while two more were abandoned by the Sikhs during their withdrawal and captured later. All 17 were placed inside the small fort at Mudki the following day, although the precaution was taken to remove their carriages so they could not be easily removed by the Sikhs if the position was subsequently lost. The morning of 19 December was also spent gathering wounded, who had been forced to spend the entire night in the open, from the battlefield.

Despite the noise of the clash carrying to Ferozeshah, no reinforcements had been sent from the main Sikh army. It is not sure where Lal Singh got to after his hasty retreat from the battlefield. Some reports suggest he hid for the remainder of the day under a bush, and then refused to send reinforcements towards the sounds of battle. A British prisoner, Captain George Bidulph, had been held in the Sikh camp during the Battle of Mudki and had noted the deteriorating mood among the soldiers. By the following morning, the Sikhs were both appalled at the inactivity of the bulk of the army the previous day and desperate to destroy Gough's force before it could link up with Littler's garrison at Ferozepore. Lal Singh was unable to demur further and sent an unspecified number of men towards Mudki. The move appears to have been nothing more than a face-saving measure on the part of Lal Singh, as Sir Harry Smith noted a 'large body of cavalry' approaching, but deemed it nothing more than a reconnaissance party. Gough, however, was concerned enough to line up his troops in what Smith dismissed as 'a

THE SIKH ARTILLERY AT MUDKI (PP. 40–41)

The Sikh artillery arm was largely discounted as a threat by the British prior to the war, but the latter learned to respect both the guns and the gunners who operated them. This illustration shows a Sikh gun crew (1) working their gun in the face of the British advance at Mudki. The Sikh gun is a 6-pdr (2), which typically had a gun crew of three to five men. Having just fired a shot, one of the men is swabbing out the barrel with a rammer (3). A second crewman, holding a linstock (4), has his thumb over the gun's vent. The third crewman (5) is carrying a roundshot to the gun for reloading, while the fourth is preparing to receive British cavalry,

drawing his long, straight sword known as a kirch (6). The gun crew are wearing the uniforms of the aspi artillery (the lighter arm of the Sikh artillery). Their headgear comprises a mixture of busby-style hats and turbans. The British cavalry (7) – comprising the 3rd Light Dragoons in their dark blue uniforms and flat white caps – is emerging from the line of the jungle in disorder, their formation broken up by the tamarisk trees and low bushes, and by the activity of Sikh snipers hidden in the trees and brush. Flashes of British artillery fire (8) can be seen through the screen of jungle, returning the fire of the Sikh guns.

very faulty position in front of Moodkee'. Some reported seeing Lal Singh himself at the head of the Sikh force. This was certainly not the case, but rumours can spread quickly among an army and there was serious concern that the main Sikh force was approaching to finish the job started the day before. Spirits in the British ranks dipped at the prospect of another hard fight immediately after the trials of the preceding day. Perhaps thinking his weak display of activity was enough to satisfy his army for now, Lal Singh almost immediately recalled his men, but Gough remained on his guard, keeping his troops in line of battle for several hours until certain that any threat had passed.

That evening, reinforcements in the form of HM 29th Foot, the 1st European Light Infantry and the 11th and 41st Native Regiments, along with a division of guns, made a welcome addition to Gough's ranks. The reinforcements had made strenuous efforts to join Gough prior to the opening of hostilities. With the 29th Foot based at Kassauli and the 1st European Light Infantry at Subathu, they had joined up at Munny Masra and marched at a rate of between 32 and 55km a day, covering an impressive 320km (200 miles) over nine days. On the evening of 18 December, they had heard the guns at Mudki but had been too far away to respond. Despite their late arrival, they were certainly made to feel welcome: regimental bands turned out to play the newcomers into the camp.

The release of Bidulph, who had been well treated by the Sikhs during his captivity, enabled him to give a thorough report on the mood of Lal Singh's army and, just as important, its dispositions around Ferozeshah. Gough therefore had a firm grasp of what he would be facing when he marched out to tackle the Sikhs again. As preparations were made, the dead being buried in mass graves while officers were allowed more private interments, an apparently small decision was taken that was to have major consequences. Sir Henry Hardinge volunteered to serve as second-in-command to Gough, and his offer was accepted. It made for a peculiar situation. As Governor General of India, Hardinge was Gough's superior. As second-in-command, he was his inferior. How each man interpreted their respective roles would be important, and this became abundantly clear just two days later.

At 4 a.m. on the morning of 21 December, with the troops having recovered from their exertions in the lead-up to Mudki and the battle itself, Gough marched his men out of their camp. The newly arrived 11th and 41st Native Regiments were left in Mudki as a garrison and word was sent to Littler at Ferozepore to bring the bulk of his 7,000 men to join Gough. The main Sikh army at Ferozeshah would be the target for the combined British force.

The resistance offered by the Sikh infantry and artillerymen was stubborn and effective, and only after hours of close-quarter combat did they withdraw from the field. (Courtesy of the Council of the National Army Museum, London)

MAJOR GENERAL SIR. R.H. SALE. G.C.B

THE BATTLE OF FEROZESHAH

Gough was never one to take his time, but there was good reason for an offensive move at this point. Most of the reinforcements within a reasonable distance had been sucked in and there was no prospect of substantial additions for at least two weeks (the 9,000 men marching from Meerut could not hope to arrive before early January). There was also no guarantee that Lal and Tej Singh could keep the lid on their soldiers' ambitions, and getting Littler out of Ferozepore was essential.

The opening miles of the march towards Ferozeshah were grim. Bodies of British soldiers dotted the landscape, many of them naked, having been stripped by locals, but Gough refused permission for their burial, insisting there was not enough time. The men marched with two days' rations, 60 rounds of ammunition and a leather-covered water bottle. Great coats had been left behind, which was a mercy during the march but promised hardship during the freezing nights to come. Tents and camp equipment had also been left behind.

Four hours after Gough set out from Mudki, Littler left Ferozepore with 5,000 men. His infantry was organized into two brigades, with HM 62nd Foot joining the 12th and 14th Native Infantry in one and the 33rd, 44th and 54th Native Infantry forming the second. A cavalry brigade numbered around 600 men, evenly divided between the 8th Native Light Cavalry and the 3rd Native Irregular Cavalry. Two field batteries and two horse artillery troops (one European and one native in each case) made up Littler's artillery. Two native regiments (the 63rd and 27th) were left to garrison Ferozepore, although a determined attack by Tej Singh could have brushed such small numbers aside without difficulty.

Gough took a wide sweep to the south of Ferozeshah to avoid triggering an action before the arrival of Littler. Although keen to take the initiative, Gough was not blind to the difficulties experienced by his men and allowed a rather leisurely pace, covering 17km in seven hours. By 11 a.m., his army was about 6km south of Ferozeshah, just south of the village of Shukoor. Here, he awaited Littler.

Intelligence from Bidulph, as well as a stream of communications from Lal Singh himself, had given Gough a clear picture of the Sikh position. It was defended on three sides, rather like a tilted rectangle with no top side. The western, southern and eastern sides of the rectangle were well defended with both men and guns. Lal Singh had done little to organize the position, and what work had been undertaken had largely been on the mens' own initiative. Still, the defensive works were formidable. The western and eastern sides were around 1,500m long, with the southern side around half that. A ditch measuring over a metre in depth and nearly two metres in breadth formed the main barrier to an attack, with the dug-out earth thrown up into a rough parapet, behind which was positioned the infantry and light guns. The Sikhs had also cleared the ground in front of their defensive works, cutting down any trees and shrubs that could offer cover to an attacking force, out to a range of around 275m. Larger guns (the Sikhs had some 62-pdrs) were installed on platforms. A total of 103 guns were arranged within the perimeter, which was much stronger on the south face and the bottom half of the western face, with the eastern face being more lightly defended.

As always, there is a range of figures offered for Sikh numbers at the battle, but it is most likely that they had around 7,000 regular infantry, 8,000 cavalry, 2,000 men to man the guns and around 7,000 other units, mostly irregulars. Within the defensive works was the village of Ferozeshah itself and a mass of tents and camp equipment from the occupying army.

The position was therefore strong, but had its weaknesses. Most obviously, the northern face of the village was undefended. Even where there were defensive works, the Sikhs had been forced to spread their numbers along 4km of entrenchments. The British could enjoy the luxury of picking one point to attack and concentrating massive numbers there to overwhelm a section of the Sikh lines. Many of the defenders, and most of the guns, could thus be rendered moot.

Gough was well aware of the layout of the defences, and he was eager to take the battle to the Sikhs, believing that he could win a victory even before Littler arrived with his substantial reinforcements. Given his experience at Mudki, he might have been expected to temper his confidence, but there were enough factors to weigh into the equation to make his opinion defensible. Strangely, though, Gough discounted his knowledge of the Sikh position and proposed a frontal assault on the southern wall of the defensive perimeter, the strongest, most heavily gunned section of the works.

A trooper, or *sowar*, of the Bengal Light Cavalry. All of the regiments of regular cavalry in the Bengal Presidency Army were officially designated light cavalry, although some were lancers. (Anne S.K. Brown Military Collection, Brown University Library)

Reasons have been offered to justify Gough's thinking. Most notably, there seems to have been concern that moving around to the north of the Sikh position would have taken time and might have prompted Tej Singh to march to join up with the main army at Ferozeshah. With Tej Singh having done nothing since crossing the Sutlej 10 days before, this seems to have been a needless concern. In the event, the decision was taken out of Gough's hands by Hardinge, who chose at this point to view himself as the Governor General rather than Gough's second-in-command. During a private conversation, he ordered Gough to await Littler's reinforcements. It was to prove a controversial decision, as it delayed the start of the battle by some hours, on the shortest day of the year.

At 1.30 p.m. the first units of Littler's force began to arrive, exhausted from their 20km march. Covering ground at a much faster rate than Gough's men (Littler had left Ferozepore four hours after Gough had marched out of Mudki), the Ferozepore contingent was in no condition for an immediate action, but Gough was impatient. Hardinge indicated that he could proceed as he wished now the army was at full strength and, allowing just a couple of hours for Littler's men to recover, Gough began to line his forces up for a frontal assault.

A 19th-century steel helmet from a Sikh warrior, complete with neck guard. Although modernization had changed the face of the Sikh Army, British units recalled facing soldiers dressed in chain mail at Ferozeshah. (Universal Images Group/Getty Images)

Sir Harry Smith, once more commanding the 1st Division, was full of scorn for Gough's preparations for the attack, claiming that the various divisional commanders were completely in the dark as to their goals. 'The army was one unwieldy battalion,' he complained, 'under one Commanding Officer who had not been granted the power of ubiquity.' Smith also claimed that he would have directed the British assault upon the eastern side of the Sikh defences, which would have left open a route of retreat towards Ferozepore and persuaded the Sikhs 'not to fight with that desperation that even bad troops will show if they are hemmed in'.

One detail in which Smith did not take issue with Gough was in relation to the lateness of the day when battle commenced; the light was already beginning to fade as the army lined up, but 'there was plenty of daylight,' Smith insisted, 'the imputation of attacking too late in the day is unfounded … although I was not then, nor am I now, an advocate for so precipitate an attack.' Smith, of course, had to keep his thoughts to himself as he took his place in the British line.

Gough's decision to attack even though the day was ending may have had one further consequence, unintended but certainly welcome. Dissatisfaction with the performance of Lal Singh was growing within the Sikh ranks and it appears there may have been a move afoot to topple him. The result of this, if an energetic, aggressive commander had replaced him, could have been dire for the British, but the sight of the red-coated infantry lining up before Ferozeshah put the issue on the back burner, for the time being at least. The Sikhs were about to get their longed-for battle. Despite this, some elements in the Sikh Army favoured a move, with at least part of their force, to take the lightly defended position at Mudki, but such thoughts came to nothing and instead the infantry and artillery calmly awaited the approach of Gough's men. The Sikh cavalry was split evenly and hovered about the north-west and north-east of the defensive works. They threatened to run down on the British at the first sign of trouble, but in the event they played no part in the battle.

Gough, with the luxury of the reinforcements from Ferozepore, was able to organize his army into four divisions. He lined three of them up for the assault and kept Smith's 1st Division as a reserve. With almost 6,000 European infantry out of a total of 18,000 men, Gough possibly had slightly higher numbers than the Sikhs, but nothing like the advantage generally preferred for an assault on prepared defences. To the left of his line he posted Littler's 4th Division, with the 12th, 14th, 33rd, 44th and 54th Native Infantry, HM 62nd Regiment of Foot, two troops of horse artillery and cavalry units comprising the 3rd Native Irregulars, the 5th and 8th Native Light Cavalry and the Governor General's Bodyguard. Littler's men faced the south-west corner of the Sikh works.

In the centre of the British line was the 3rd Division, commanded by Brigadier-General Wallace. Significantly weaker than Littler's division, Wallace commanded only three native regiments (the 2nd, 26th and 73rd Native Grenadier Regiments) and HM 9th Foot.

The strongest division, Major-General Gilbert's 2nd Division, would tackle the weaker section of the Sikh lines. The 16th Native Grenadiers, 1st European Light Infantry and 41st and 45th Native Infantry were joined by HM 29th and 80th Foot. A cavalry contingent, under Brigadier White, saw the 3rd Light Dragoons combined with the 4th Native Light Cavalry (lancers).

Some sources claim Gough divided his 69 guns and two howitzers fairly evenly along the British line (they were mostly comprised of light pieces and were seriously overmatched by the bigger Sikh weaponry). Sir Harry Smith, however, claimed that the guns were largely massed in the centre of the line, and noted that the two brigades of his reserve division were divided by this artillery formation, which he described as stretching over a kilometre.

As at Mudki, it was left to the artillery to open the battle. From a range of 1,100 yards the Sikhs responded to British mortar fire, and 300 yards closer the British guns began to fire. It was an uneven contest. Whereas at Mudki the British artillery had been unable to make superior numbers count, here they were definitively outclassed. Witnesses attest to the fact that the Sikhs fired at a considerably higher rate, three shots for every two they received in reply, and they also regularly loaded their sturdier guns with double shot. Smith would go out of his way to defend the performance of the British gunners, insisting they had been badly used by Gough, 'hence the mortality and wrongly imputed inefficiency of that arm, a noble arm when called forth in its legitimate field'. Whatever the reasons, however, the result was the British artillery took a fearful mauling and most of Gough's guns were knocked out of action. 'We had not a gun left,' noted Colonel James Robertson of HM 31st Foot, 'most of them were smashed, and dead horses and broken limbers were lying about, having been completely outmatched by the heavier artillery of the Sikhs.'

Having failed to achieve anything with his artillery, Gough turned to the bayonet and ordered Littler's 4th Division to advance. The Sikh artillery hammered the advancing lines, switching to grape as the range decreased, until only 150 yards separated the opposing lines. In Littler's own words, 'the casualties were awful'. His sole British regiment, the 62nd Foot, found

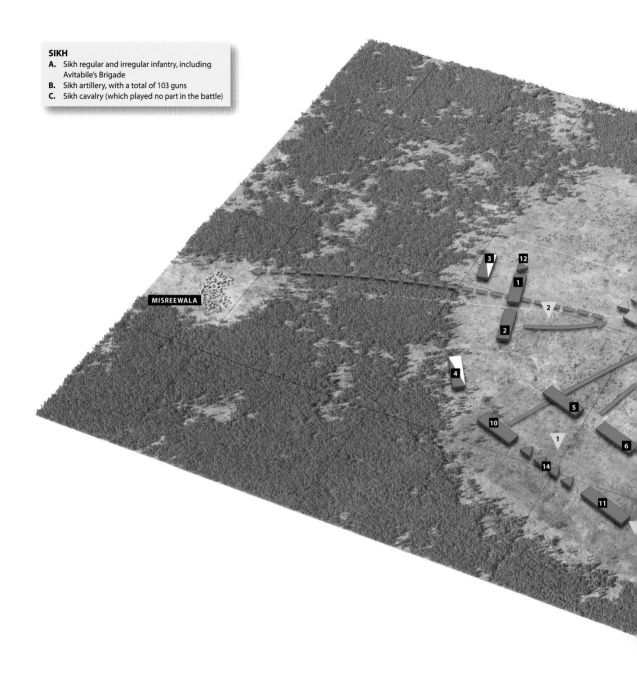

SIKH
- **A.** Sikh regular and irregular infantry, including Avitabile's Brigade
- **B.** Sikh artillery, with a total of 103 guns
- **C.** Sikh cavalry (which played no part in the battle)

MISREEWALA

▼ EVENTS

1. Following a one-sided artillery contest, Gough orders his infantry to advance.

2. Littler's 4th Division attacks first, but is repulsed by determined Sikh defence. After moving forward again, it falls back in disarray to Misreewala, taking no further part in the battle.

3. The 3rd and 2nd divisions, personally led by Hardinge and Gough, attack the south and eastern faces of the Sikh position, respectively.

4. The 3rd Light Dragoons mount an effective but costly charge into the Sikh camp.

5. Smith leads a brigade of his reserve division deep into the Sikh camp, but becomes detached from the rest of the British force as night falls.

6. Sikh units converge on Smith's amalgamated force of around 3,000 men and he is forced to withdraw.

7. The British take refuge in a huge, confused rectangle and are fired upon by the exultant Sikhs throughout the night.

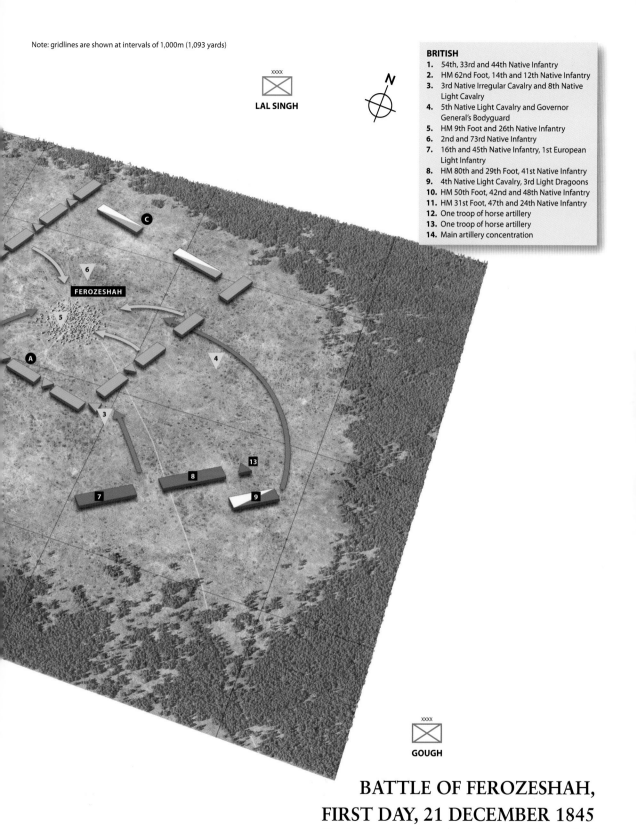

Note: gridlines are shown at intervals of 1,000m (1,093 yards)

LAL SINGH

N

BRITISH
1. 54th, 33rd and 44th Native Infantry
2. HM 62nd Foot, 14th and 12th Native Infantry
3. 3rd Native Irregular Cavalry and 8th Native Light Cavalry
4. 5th Native Light Cavalry and Governor General's Bodyguard
5. HM 9th Foot and 26th Native Infantry
6. 2nd and 73rd Native Infantry
7. 16th and 45th Native Infantry, 1st European Light Infantry
8. HM 80th and 29th Foot, 41st Native Infantry
9. 4th Native Light Cavalry, 3rd Light Dragoons
10. HM 50th Foot, 42nd and 48th Native Infantry
11. HM 31st Foot, 47th and 24th Native Infantry
12. One troop of horse artillery
13. One troop of horse artillery
14. Main artillery concentration

FEROZESHAH

GOUGH

BATTLE OF FEROZESHAH, FIRST DAY, 21 DECEMBER 1845
The battle took place near the towns of Ferozeshah and Misreewala.

itself advancing alone as the native regiments had fallen back. Eventually, the 62nd ground to a halt and began to fall back itself. In this first advance, the regiment had lost more than a hundred dead and suffered nearly 200 further casualties. Some men appear to have actually reached the Sikh defences, or perhaps some impetuous Sikhs had left their works to attack, as several British officers were later found with sabre wounds.

Only one of Littler's two brigades appears to have engaged the enemy, the three sepoy regiments of Brigadier Ashburnham taking no casualties at all. This may explain Sir Harry Smith's assessment that Littler's attack, 'appeared to me one of no weight from its formation'. As Smith feared, the attack failed, as did a second. The 4th Division had been knocked out of the battle. Matters could have been worse, as it appeared the inert Sikh cavalry might be ordered against the ragged remains of Littler's men. Squares were formed in anticipation of this, but no such charge came and the 4th Division was allowed to withdraw from the battlefield, taking refuge at Misreewala, about 3km distant.

It seems possible that Littler had advanced prematurely, as his assault was mostly over before the other two sections of the British line got under way. When the centre and right divisions moved into action, they enjoyed far greater success. On the right, the division of Major-General Gilbert advanced on the south-east corner of the Sikh positions. Brigadier-General Taylor's brigade initially moved forward in echelon, with HM 29th Foot on the extreme right leading the way. HM 80th Foot could not be restrained, however, and moved forward of their position in the advance until they were almost in line with the 29th. The regiments reached the defensive works and broke through, only to find Sikh infantry awaiting them. Pushing the defenders back, the 80th then encountered a Sikh regiment dressed incongruously in chain mail. Although it can only be guessed how uncomfortable such armour was in the heat and dust, this regiment nevertheless put up determined resistance before it was driven back.

The second brigade of Gilbert's division held its fire as it advanced, although taking casualties at every step from the Sikh guns. As they neared the line, the order was given to charge and the brigade quickly closed with the Sikh artillery, although the air was so thick with smoke it was described as being like night. A primitive abatis of chopped branches had been laid before the defensive works, but this did little to hinder the assault. The performance of the Sikh infantry at this stage was mixed. First appearing calm, an organized line dropped to one knee to deliver a volley into the troops advancing upon them, but then they became disorganized as the British charged, with many men retreating rapidly while

Major George Broadfoot, the political agent, fell while attacking a Sikh battery on the first day of the battle. Having been shot from his horse, he quickly remounted, charged again, and was shot through the heart. His body was not discovered until the second day of the battle. (©TopFoto.co.uk)

DEATH OF MAJOR BROADFOOT.

some stayed to fight it out. The 2nd Division was therefore able to penetrate the Sikh line and pushed the defenders back into the camp itself.

Wallace's relatively weak 3rd Division, advancing in the middle of the British line, had little idea where it was heading thanks to the choking dust and smoke from the Sikh guns. The only British regiment in the formation, HM 9th Foot, on the left of the division, walked directly up to the Sikh guns and took heavy casualties, before the regiment rallied and overran the position.

Accounts vary on when Smith's reserve troops were thrown into the fray. In his own reports he suggests Hardinge (commanding in the centre) called for his men as soon as Littler's assault began to fail, but others suggest it was only when the 2nd and 3rd divisions had made it to the Sikh lines that he was called on, by Gough, to drive home the advantage. Reports from Wallace's 3rd Division claim that Smith's men were already in possession of the village when their attack reached that point, making it seem most likely that he was ordered into action very early on, but the confusion of the battle leaves room for doubt. Smith also reported that the divided nature of his position (his division being separated by the huge artillery formation) meant he could only lead one of his brigades forward, although the other advanced too, possibly under its own initiative.

Smith recalled British and native troops falling back as his men advanced, hampering his progress, and he reported a storm of shot and musket fire as his men tried to make their way to the Sikh lines. 'The balls at first came popping past just like cricket-balls at play,' noted Colonel Robertson. 'Then an ugly shot came whiz, and hit my right-hand man fair in the face, and I heard a man exclaim, "There's poor Finnigan down!"' Visibility was appalling, and Smith received word that four battalions of Avitabile's Brigade were heading for him, but in the confusion it is unclear if these formidable troops ever engaged Smith's men. Regardless, the British units stood their ground and returned fire as best they could, although with little or no idea where their enemy was. 'The gallant old 50th bore the whole brunt,' Smith recalled proudly, 'opening a rapid fire.' Despite the stoicism of his men, however, Smith feared that he was about to be repulsed and resorted to a bayonet charge, which saw his men established in the Sikh defences.

On the right, the 3rd Light Dragoons charged to back up Gilbert's advance, making it into the Sikh camp itself. Here they encountered much the same treatment as they had received at Mudki. Whereas in the previous battle it was jungle that hampered their movements, at Ferozeshah it was tents and camp equipment. The result was identical: the cavalry were unable to move freely or at pace and became easy targets for Sikh snipers. The 3rd Light Dragoons took disastrous casualties, with two-thirds of them falling dead or injured. Still, the determination of the British attack was bearing fruit, as the Sikhs stubbornly gave ground. Smith's men penetrated deep into the camp, but this brought distractions for men who had now been tormented by heat and dust all day and had not had a drink for hours. Many broke off their attack to search for water.

The scene within the Sikh lines had become nightmarish, with fires springing up at all points and ammunition exploding randomly. As night fell, cohesion broke down almost entirely and fighting became sporadic and unfocused. One brigade of Smith's 1st Division had made it all the way to the village of Ferozeshah when the Sikhs rallied and began to push back.

Gough saw the futility of continuing the attack and took the decision to recall his men. In the chaos, however, it was impossible for his order to reach everyone. Smith, in fact, believed that the battle was won. He was aware of Littler's repulse, but, 'the victory appeared complete on my right; crowds of advancing, straggling officers and soldiers came up and I resolved again to push forward'. Smith found himself with a hodgepodge force that he estimated at around 3,000 men, made from any number of regiments, and he calmly awaited the arrival of the rest of the army to seal the triumph. Instead, it was Sikh units that began to converge on his position, which became tenuous in the extreme as the moon rose, bathing the field in a light that Smith described as being as bright as day.

The British and native soldiers were by now so exhausted, many simply fell asleep and some were even killed by advancing Sikhs as they lay oblivious to their peril. When the enemy manoeuvred a gun to threaten the rear of Smith's force, he recognized that it was time to leave. With the Sikhs calling out and taunting the apparently trapped soldiers, Smith faked an attack and then fell back, following a macabre trail of dead and dying soldiers all the way to Misreewala, where he found the shattered remains of Littler's division. There was talk of retiring to Ferozepore, but Smith was unwilling to leave the field completely. 'The Commander-in-Chief with his army is not far from us,' he retorted, 'meditating an attack as soon as it is daylight, and find him I will if in hell, where I will join him, rather than make one retrograde step till I have ascertained some fact.' It was a neat little outburst, and possibly more eloquent in the remembering than it was at the time, but the matter was soon pressed by one of Gough's aides, who insisted the move

The 3rd Light Dragoons were in the thick of the action once more at Ferozeshah, staging an effective but costly charge into the Sikh position, through the line of defences to the east of their camp. (Anne S.K. Brown Military Collection, Brown University Library)

to Ferozepore was necessary. When asked why, he stated simply, 'Oh, the army has been beaten.'

Gough's men had not yet been beaten, but the outcome of the battle was in serious doubt. The bulk of the men had formed up in a vast rectangle after withdrawing from Ferozeshah. While Sir Harry Smith had believed the battle had been won, most others in the army were convinced it had been lost. Sikh drums played through the night and any attempt to light a fire drew an instant reaction from Sikh snipers and guns, so the men huddled in freezing conditions, driven nearly mad with thirst and hunger. Colonel Robertson spent the night sandwiched between a pair of accommodating soldiers and dreamt of swimming in a 'beautiful bath' and 'drinking mouthfuls of water'. His dream was to come true, more or less, the next day.

The night, however, was one of doubt and foreboding. The Sikhs could almost certainly have completed the destruction of Gough's army, but having reoccupied their lines by 1 a.m., they failed to push on and attack the disorganized defensive rectangle. British troops lay down wherever they were, with no attempt to find their respective regiments, and a determined charge by the Sikhs would surely have led to a complete victory, but with no strong leadership, the Sikhs contented themselves with taunting their opponents and looking forward to a glorious victory the next morning.

Gough's decision to 'march light' from Mudki now came back to haunt him, as his men had no greatcoats or tents to make the night bearable, and water and provisions had also been left behind. Sporadic artillery fire from the Sikh guns made rest difficult, but the men were so exhausted many simply slept through. Occasional sorties were made to silence the Sikh guns, but little impact was made, and the Sikhs fell into a pattern of allowing a period of calm, then opening fire and sounding their kettle drums at the same time to startle the British soldiers awake.

The situation appeared desperate, if not already lost, and several officers beseeched Gough to withdraw under cover of darkness. Either of Ferozepore or Mudki promised relief if the army could make it there safely, but Gough was unwilling to budge, convinced that he could fight and win the next day. A withdrawal was far from an easy option anyway. With the men too exhausted to march, it could have degenerated into chaos and invited an attack from the Sikhs. The curiously inactive Sikh cavalry, in particular, could have sprung into life at any moment.

If withdrawing was impossible, the army would have to stand and fight again the next day. There was little doubt that Gough would order another assault, and some officers took the opportunity to get their affairs in order. Messages were sent to Mudki to destroy official documents, while Hardinge ordered his son to leave. There seemed to be little hope left, before an extraordinary turn of events renewed it.

At some time in the night, certainly before dawn, a by now familiar lull in the Sikh artillery fire stretched out longer than usual. Lal Singh had started to withdraw some of his men. Infantry and gun crews were pulled out of the line, leaving the defences in a greatly weakened state. It remains a mystery why the Sikh soldiers accepted these baffling orders at a time when a complete and stunning victory was so clearly within their grasp. Discipline had certainly been breaking down as they became increasingly disenchanted, even suspicious, of the actions of their officers. Lal Singh's tent had been ransacked during the night and rumblings about replacing him had begun

days earlier at Mudki. Yet, as Gough's army huddled together in the vast rectangle that would have made an irresistible target once the sun came up, the Sikh soldiers accepted an order to withdraw from their lines. The unruly nature of the Sikh Army was one of the primary reasons for the war breaking out in the first place, but now they obeyed an order that simply made no sense. To make matters worse, the Sikhs left huge amounts of supplies behind, as if they were the ones being driven from the battlefield in disorder. Attempts were made to spoil the water supply, with bodies thrown into wells, but these were hasty and uncoordinated. Lal Singh had somehow convinced his men to act as if they were the ones who needed to extricate themselves from the field as quickly as possible. Only a determined few remained, unwilling to give up their hard-earned victory, but the extensive Sikh lines were manned by hundreds, rather than thousands, when the sun started to rise once more.

Most accounts of the following day's fighting are brief. The treachery of the Sikh leadership was not widely known at the time, which colours many of the personal accounts of the battle. Time after time, therefore, accounts of the harrowing fighting of 21 December are followed by the walkover presented to Gough's men the following day with no comment or apparent puzzlement. Sir Harry Smith simply said the attack 'was now carried without a check'. Colonel Robertson recounted how 'in a very short time we had possession of the camp'. The fighting was limited following the British advance (the attack started at 7 a.m.) but where Sikhs remained in the line, they resisted fiercely. Robertson presented a graphic image of a British infantryman losing four fingers from the sword of a Sikh soldier he was in the process of running through with his bayonet.

A limited amount of supplies had arrived from Mudki early in the morning and some of the attacking soldiers had gulped down a ration of grog, but they needed no Dutch courage against the depleted Sikh defences. In fact, the major issue became one of retaining order as Gough's men began to run amuck in the largely deserted Sikh camp. There was no time for discernment as the soldiers ran through the tents, driven wild with hunger and thirst. Colonel Robertson grabbed the first bucket he could find, which had been used to rinse off the sponges of a Sikh gun crew and was therefore filled with filthy water, and upended it. The water was 'black as ink', but he swallowed as much as he could before he was seized with a violent pain in his stomach. Not having drunk for hours (and perhaps because the water was generously mixed with filth from the barrel of a cannon), Robertson described the sensation as being 'as if I had swallowed a sword'. He faired better at a well, although the press for water meant he was nearly pushed in (and several men throughout the camp did meet with this fate). A supply of oranges was also devoured with relish, and the remainder of the haul was carried away for his men, bundled up in the trousers of a dead soldier.

Due to the condition of the men, the terrible losses they had taken the previous day and the disorganization caused by the sudden appearance of large amounts of food and water, there was no chance of pursuing the withdrawing Sikh Army, nor was there much appetite for it. A victory had been handed to the British when a decisive defeat had seemed likely, and there was a sense of unreality about the dramatic change of fortune. A day that had started with the men licking dew from the barrels of their guns had turned into a rampage through the plentiful supplies of the Sikh camp.

The sudden arrival of another Sikh force punctured this happy bubble. Tej Singh had finally marched from Ferozepore and now lined up, apparently to challenge ownership of Ferozeshah once more. Sir Harry Smith, unaware of the true reason behind the poor leadership of Tej Singh and Lal Singh, had credited the inactivity of the latter to the skill with which Littler had evacuated Ferozepore. Tej Singh, Smith believed, had been tricked into thinking the garrison was still in position and had only marched to Ferozeshah once he had discovered his mistake. In fact, Tej Singh had been waging a mighty struggle to keep his hands on the reins of his army, while his men agitated for him to march to the sound of the guns, first at Mudki and then, closer and louder, at Ferozeshah.

Tej Singh had pulled off a minor miracle in restraining his men long enough to keep them out of the first day's fighting at Ferozeshah. Their arrival would have provided exactly the sort of fresh units needed to sweep Gough's army away, but it remains far from certain that Tej Singh would not have somehow managed to prevent them from attacking, so the matter is not clear-cut. What does seem clear is that even arriving late, on the morning of 22 December, Tej Singh's men presented a serious threat to Gough's disorganized army.

Even with the odds so finely balanced, one of Gough's officers was able to appreciate the majestic appearance of the newly arrived Sikh Army. 'A glorious sun at our back played on a truly magnificent advancing line of artillery, infantry and cavalry, a mile in length,' wrote Captain Henry Palmer, an officer in the 48th Native Infantry. 'Richly dressed Sikh officers, colours and bands all glittering. It was a pretty sight.'

Pretty it may have been, but if Tej Singh had rethought his allegiance it could also have been deadly. The exhausted British and native troops dragged themselves into a makeshift defensive line, with some troops ordered to form squares in anticipation of a cavalry charge. Ammunition for what remained of the British artillery was scarce and an effort was made to find cannonballs in the Sikh camp, but with most of their cannon having been of significantly larger calibre than the British guns, most of it was unusable. As the artillery in Tej Singh's army moved forward and opened fire, the British resorted to firing unloaded guns to give at least an appearance of defiance.

Once more there were serious forebodings of imminent disaster. Colonel Robertson later recalled how Sir Henry Hardinge rode into his infantry square and delivered a little pep talk to the men of the 31st Regiment. 'Thirty-First,' he said, 'I was with you when you saved the battle of Albuera; behave like men now.' Despite the apparent desperate nature of the situation, Robertson then fell asleep, while the Sikh artillery pounded the British formations and Gough's guns barked their toothless replies. He awoke to see a small band of the 3rd Light Dragoons, supported by a part of the 4th Native Light Cavalry, making a charge at the Sikh Army. The British troops cheered this act of gallantry, but when the native cavalry broke and fell back, they actually opened fire on them in disgust. Then, as Robertson watched, the dust from this little cavalry action cleared to reveal the Sikh Army in retreat.

Tej Singh, with no intention of exploiting his dominant position, somehow convinced his men to walk away from what would have been a near-certain victory. Robertson believed he must have received a huge bribe to act in such a fashion, and it is unclear how he convinced his men to retreat under such favourable circumstances. Sir Harry Smith, ever confident, believed that Tej Singh's army would have been 'easy prey' for the British had they not been so utterly exhausted, and it is no doubt true that the British and native regiments would have defended their entrenchments, inherited from the Sikhs, with bravery and stubbornness, but it is impossible to imagine anything other than a Sikh victory had Tej Singh committed his men to an attack. At the time, with few aware of Tej Singh's duplicity, excuses were

With the bulk of the Sikh defenders having pulled out of their positions overnight, British troops including the 31st Foot found progress much easier on the second day of the battle. (Anne S.K. Brown Military Collection, Brown University Library)

dreamed up to explain his inexplicable behaviour. Most commonly cited is the unauthorized withdrawal of some British horse artillery (the officer responsible was court-martialled, but not punished as he was believed to be suffering from sunstroke at the time). This movement towards Ferozepore, some claimed, may have convinced Tej Singh that the British were attempting to outflank him, or at least given him a pretext for withdrawal. It would have been a flimsy excuse, but the retreat of the Sikhs was so unfathomable it was certain to spawn such theories.

After remaining in position for an hour or so, in case Tej Singh changed his mind, the British soldiers were allowed to fall out and enjoy the delights of the Sikh camp. Plentiful food and plunder kept them happily occupied for the rest of the day, although there were still dangers. Some Sikh soldiers had hidden in tents and ambushed British and sepoy troops when they entered in search of loot. There was also a substantial number of mines buried throughout the camp, which periodically killed or wounded a soldier or two. In one spectacular incident a wagon of ammunition triggered a mine, resulting in a huge explosion that killed men and horses over a wide area. Teams were organized to search for these deadly devices and around 100 were eventually found and made safe, although they were still claiming lives two days after the battle, on Christmas Eve.

The two-day Battle of Ferozeshah had been a costly affair for both sides, with casualties again reckoned to have been about equal. Gough's penchant for frontal assaults saw 694 of his men killed, with a further 1,721 wounded. Sikh losses were difficult to assess as many men no doubt died of

The Sikhs left huge quantities of supplies and ordnance in their camp after their hasty withdrawal, which was fallen upon with desperation by the exhausted British forces. (Anne S.K. Brown Military Collection, Brown University Library)

THE CAPTURE OF FEROZESHAH (PP. 58–59)

Following fierce fighting the previous day, the battered remains of the British Army found the Sikh positions had been mostly evacuated during the night and they captured the camp with little resistance the following morning. This scene shows the British and native troops spilling into the Sikh camp, fighting with the few Sikh soldiers who had remained at their posts, searching for food and drink and engaging in plundering. The camp was made up of tents (1), mostly of a tepee style, with some larger ones; coloured stripes denoted a tent belonging to an officer. The camp was in a state of chaos, as the Sikhs withdrew without taking any of their equipment with them. The British troops, some of whom were from the 9th (in taller shakos, and yellow colours and cuffs) and 31st regiments, were so intent on rifling through baggage

and tents that they fell victim to hidden dangers. Sikh snipers (2) were hidden inside some of the tents, and one British soldier has just been shot. The Sikhs also mined the camp extensively and a large explosion has just taken place in the background (3). Bengal irregular cavalrymen (4) can be seen riding through the camp searching for hidden Sikh soldiers. Native (sepoy) troops are also shown (5), dressed in much the same manner as the British regiments. One episode mentioned in accounts of the battle is also depicted here, involving a well (6). The British troops, driven nearly mad by thirst, crowded around the well and used a pair of trousers, with the legs knotted at the ends, as a makeshift bucket. With no protective wall around the well, it would have been easy for men to fall in (7).

their wounds during their withdrawal. Most agreed that they had taken no more losses than the British Army and the battle came to be viewed as, if anything, a Sikh victory.

Thankfully, reinforcements were on their way to Gough's battered army. A siege train was plodding its way from Delhi, guarded by two native infantry regiments. It was a fat, tempting target, with the column sprawling over 16km, and active Sikh leadership could and should have seen it targeted. Even if all went smoothly, however, it was not expected to arrive until well into the new year.

Following the Battle of Ferozeshah, Gough had moved his men to Sobraon, carefully following the line of the Sikh withdrawal but unable to initiate any sort of offensive action until his army was strengthened. The addition of around 10,000 fresh troops under Sir John Grey, on 6 January, was a great relief. Grey's men included HM 100th Foot, as well as the 9th and 16th Lancers, the 3rd Native Light Cavalry, a pair of native regiments and artillery. It was a substantial boost to Gough's strength.

More distant, the men under Sir Charles Napier were on their way from Sind, along with 60 guns, and smaller packets of men were still being soaked up from the rest of the region. It would strengthen the British force, but was also turning the contest into an all-or-nothing gambit. A serious defeat, having sucked in so many resources, would be catastrophic.

The food and drink enjoyed by the British following their hard-earned success at Ferozeshah was, of course, now denied to the Sikhs, and Lal Singh's army began to suffer seriously from shortages. Resupply ought to have been straightforward, and would have been had it not been for the forces working against the army. Gulab Singh, who had carefully kept his own men out of the hostilities, was now organizing the supply of the army and was deliberately dragging his feet, sending only small quantities to the front. The soldiers sent representatives to the Sikh court at Lahore to beg for the support they needed, but were met with derision. Maharani Jindan at one point removed her petticoat, threw it at a party of soldiers and called them cowards. It was brutal treatment for men who by now were becoming increasingly suspicious over the leadership they were receiving. When materiel did arrive at their camp, much of it was found to be useless, and bags of gunpowder were often found to contain nothing but sand. It was a confusing and frustrating time for the soldiers, but they had soured relations with their own officers to such an extent that they had no means of redress.

The pause in hostilities had come at just the right moment for the British. An outbreak of dysentery had hit the men, in many cases the result of drinking contaminated water in the Sikh camp at Ferozeshah. As they recovered, the army was steadily reinforced and resupplied, and thoughts turned to a resumption of the offensive. On 7 January, Gough moved his men closer to the Sikh position, but not so close as to trigger a response. He was not yet ready to fight again. The village of Bootewala became the new base for the British, about 8km away from Lal Singh.

Desperate to take the offensive, the Sikh soldiers were finally satisfied when Lal Singh agreed to once more cross the Sutlej. However, he split his army, leaving half of it on the north bank while the remainder crossed to challenge Gough's army. It was as transparent a ploy as could be imagined to weaken his position, and he once more took up a strictly defensive posture. Lal Singh's men were by now in no doubt that he was at least incompetent, and he was dragged bodily across the bridge to the south side of the Sutlej so that he might be forced to stand with his men. Had genuine treachery been suspected, it is difficult to imagine that he would not have been executed on the spot, so he must somehow have managed to disguise his true intentions, although suspicions were rising.

The Sikh position was faulty as well. The defensive entrenchments at Sobraon, commanded by Tej Singh, did not extend fully to the Sutlej on their right flank, leaving a wide gap that could be exploited by enemy forces. To make sure the British were aware of this, messengers were sent to Ferozepore and Gough also received independent intelligence from his own spies.

With Sir Henry Hardinge in command at Ferozepore, preparations were being made for a crossing of the Sutlej using the boats that had been prepared the previous year. Although they had been sunk just prior to the outbreak of hostilities, it had been done in such a way that they could easily be repaired. At a section of the river where it was split into three streams by sand bars, a bridge was constructed over the larger, 600ft span (the other two streams were easily fordable). The British were almost ready to renew the contest.

THE BATTLE OF BHUDOWAL

Transporting 10,000 men across the Sutlej was no minor operation and would have involved the use of ferries, boats and fords. The river would then make it extremely difficult to withdraw a defeated army in good order, as the Sikhs found to their cost at Aliwal and Sobraon. (G.T. Vigne/ Royal Geographical Society/ Getty Images)

The situation, however, was about to be shaken up considerably, because the British were not the only ones who could call up fresh troops. Eastwards, towards Ludhiana, the soldiers under Ranjodh Singh, who had sat quietly at Phillaur for the opening moves of the war, finally swung into action. Numbering around 10,000 men, including some 2,000 irregular cavalry, this was a substantial force. Equally important was the fact that Ranjodh Singh does not appear to have been involved in any sort of treachery against his men. Cruelly for the Sikhs, he was also lacking in military skill. Still, with a respectable artillery arm of 70 guns, Ranjodh Singh could cause problems, especially if he moved with energy to tackle isolated British positions one by one.

The build-up to Aliwal, 17–26 January 1846

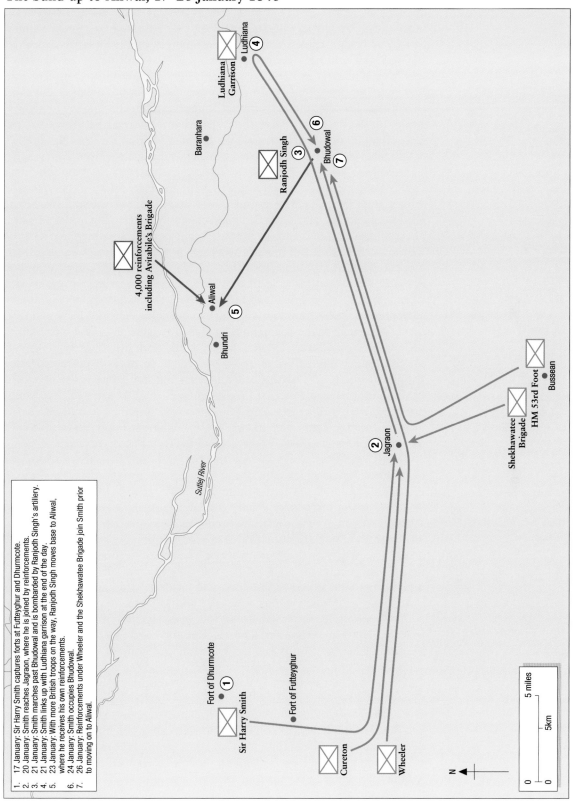

1. 17 January: Sir Harry Smith captures forts at Futteyghur and Dhurmcote.
2. 20 January: Smith reaches Jagraon, where he is joined by reinforcements.
3. 21 January: Smith marches past Bhudowal and is bombarded by Ranjodh Singh's artillery.
4. 21 January: Smith links up with Ludhiana garrison at the end of the day.
5. 23 January: With more British troops on the way, Ranjodh Singh moves base to Aliwal, where he receives his own reinforcements.
6. 24 January: Smith occupies Bhudowal.
7. 26 January: Reinforcements under Wheeler and the Shekhawatee Brigade join Smith prior to moving on to Aliwal.

Ludhiana, with a small British garrison, was the obvious first target, and civilians began to stream out of the city as soon as this latest Sikh formation crossed the Sutlej. Ranjodh Singh was quickly bolstered by a small number of reinforcements under Ajeet Singh (unique among the Sikh rajas south of the Sutlej in fighting against the British), who had already staged a minor attack on Ludhiana earlier in the month. Having finally sprung into activity, however, this new piece on the chessboard moved in the opposite direction to that expected by most observers. Rather than descending on Ludhiana, it moved away from it, taking up a defensive posture at Bhudowal, where it threatened nobody. There was also the possibility of it retrieving supplies from a Sikh-held fort at Dhurmcote, which prompted a response from Gough.

Unable to leave such a substantial force unmolested, as Ranjodh Singh might at any moment decide to start using it, Sir Harry Smith was despatched with a small force to first capture the fort at Dhurmcote and another at Futteyghur. Smith was no doubt a good choice for such a detached command. He was brave, active and level-headed, but he was also highly critical of Gough's generalship and it is possible the commander-in-chief was ready for a break. Smith had been free with his criticism of Gough's dispositions at Sobraon, submitting his ideas on how the army should be lined up along with an explanatory letter. Gough, according to Smith, eventually adopted this new arrangement, but it took him 48 hours to put it into effect. On 16 January, Smith was called to the commander-in-chief and given his mission to capture the two enemy positions. He was to take a brigade of his division, along with the 3rd Native Light Cavalry and a number of troopers from the corps of irregular cavalry. A lively bit of verbal sparring saw Smith insist he would finish the job within a day, while Gough smiled and suggested that would not be possible as the forts were 26 miles away. 'What I say shall be,' Smith insisted, 'provided that the officer and the Engineers supply me in time with the powder I want to blow in the gates in the case of necessity.'

Smith's confidence was borne out, as he found the first position, at Futteyghur, unoccupied and the second in no mood for resistance. A brief bombardment with 9-pdrs and a howitzer saw the small garrison at Dhurmcote surrender. While contemplating his success with some satisfaction, Smith was alerted that reinforcements were on the way to him. The 16th Lancers, the rest of the irregular horse and two troops of horse artillery (comprising 12 guns) were on their way to join him and he was then to march towards Jagraon. Ranjodh Singh's army was overestimated at 30,000, but Smith betrayed no misgivings about marching towards it with just a brigade of infantry, one of cavalry and 18 guns.

On 19 January, Smith set off without even awaiting his reinforcements. Sending word to Brigadier Charles Robert Cureton, commanding the reinforcing cavalry units, to meet him at Jagraon, he pushed on. The protection of the siege train marching from Delhi was Smith's primary goal, and it was hoped that the 53rd Foot would be able to join him from Bussean. Lieutenant-Colonel Philips, commanding the 53rd, asked for a day's leeway in marching to Jagraon, but Smith insisted he move out immediately, as the garrison at Ludhiana was still believed to be a possible target for Ranjodh Singh. On 20 January, Smith arrived at Jagraon and was joined by the cavalry and guns sent by Gough and the 53rd Regiment. Smith now called for the garrison at Ludhiana to march towards Bhudowal and set off on the 21st to meet them.

Despite Smith's innate confidence, it was clear Ranjodh Singh's army was too strong to consider attacking before bringing in all available manpower, so Smith planned to give it a wide berth on the way to linking up with the Ludhiana garrison. However, something went badly wrong and when his column passed the village of Bhudowal, he found that he was within range of the Sikh guns. The reason for the mistake is not clear, but Smith believed it was down to his Indian scouts. Believing they had deliberately led him too close to Bhudowal, he had them executed, but not before the miscalculation had led to considerable loss among his men.

Marching across the face of the Sikh position, artillery fire hit the men at an angle. Colonel Roberts of the 31st noted how he saw one shot kill seven soldiers as they marched by under 'a heavy and most destructive fire'. Although his men were in no position to assault the Sikh defences, being already tired from their long march, Smith felt he had to respond when the Sikhs threw a line of seven battalions across the rear of his column and looked about to attack. He seriously contemplated an offensive move and even began to line his men up, when Roberts heard him mutter, 'It won't do today; they are too strong for us.'

Yet again, a lack of water was tormenting the marching British, who drank thirstily from a muddy pool that they passed on their march. Forcing down the water, which Roberts described as being 'almost as thick as soup,' the men were almost instantly violently sick. The baggage train then became detached in the confusion and was ransacked by Sikh cavalry, while many men fell back on Jagraon. Already operating with limited forces, Smith lost 69 dead, 68 wounded and a further 77 missing during the Battle of Bhudowal. Once more, however, Sikh cavalry had not been unleashed, except to plunder the baggage train, and Smith was able to join up with the Ludhiana garrison.

Even so, the cumulative effect of the regular battles was being felt. The siege train from Delhi halted as rumours began to circulate about the British

A model of the Sikh fort at Phillaur, base of Ranjodh Singh prior to his crossing of the Sutlej. Completed in 1809 to counter the British fortress at Ludhiana, it is now home to the Punjab Police Academy. (Photo by Inderjit Singh)

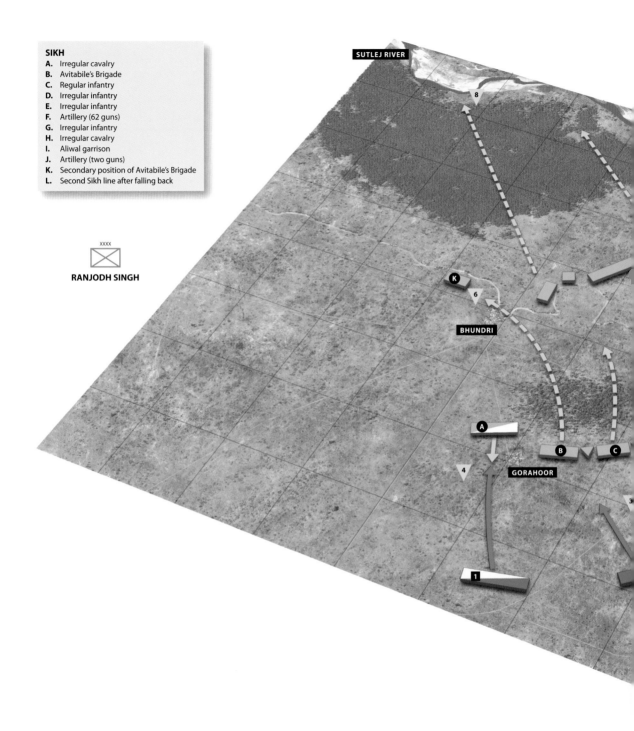

SIKH

A. Irregular cavalry
B. Avitabile's Brigade
C. Regular infantry
D. Irregular infantry
E. Irregular infantry
F. Artillery (62 guns)
G. Irregular infantry
H. Irregular cavalry
I. Aliwal garrison
J. Artillery (two guns)
K. Secondary position of Avitabile's Brigade
L. Second Sikh line after falling back

RANJODH SINGH

SUTLEJ RIVER

BHUNDRI

GORAHOOR

EVENTS

1. The brigades of Godby and Hicks advance on the lightly defended village of Aliwal.

2. British cavalry on the right flank repulses its Sikh opposition and Aliwal is captured.

3. The brigades of Wheeler and Wilson advance against the strongest Sikh units.

4. British cavalry establishes dominance over its Sikh opponents on the left flank.

5. With their position threatened by the British troops at Aliwal, the Sikh irregulars fall back.

6. Avitabile's regulars withdraw in good order though heavily pressed by British cavalry.

7. The Sikhs manage to establish a second defensive line.

8. The second line breaks and Sikh units are pursued to the banks of the Sutlej.

Note: gridlines are shown at intervals of 1,000m (1,093 yards)

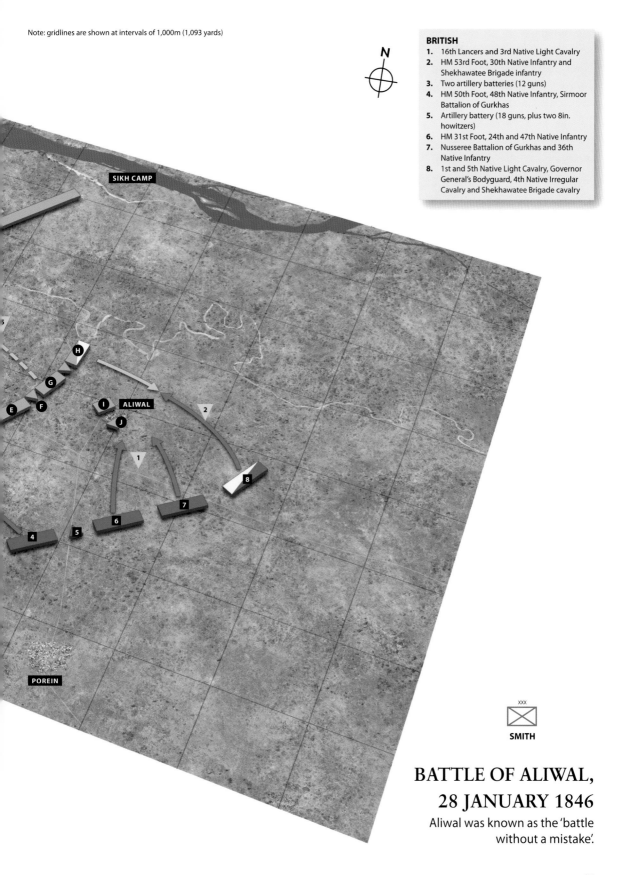

BRITISH
1. 16th Lancers and 3rd Native Light Cavalry
2. HM 53rd Foot, 30th Native Infantry and Shekhawatee Brigade infantry
3. Two artillery batteries (12 guns)
4. HM 50th Foot, 48th Native Infantry, Sirmoor Battalion of Gurkhas
5. Artillery battery (18 guns, plus two 8in. howitzers)
6. HM 31st Foot, 24th and 47th Native Infantry
7. Nusseree Battalion of Gurkhas and 36th Native Infantry
8. 1st and 5th Native Light Cavalry, Governor General's Bodyguard, 4th Native Irregular Cavalry and Shekhawatee Brigade cavalry

SIKH CAMP

ALIWAL

POREIN

xxx
SMITH

BATTLE OF ALIWAL, 28 JANUARY 1846

Aliwal was known as the 'battle without a mistake'.

having met with a disaster. There was a sense of uncertainty in the region and a feeling that the Sikhs might be about to prevail. A solid British victory was needed to restore confidence and a full-scale confrontation between Smith and Ranjodh Singh was inevitable. Its outcome could swing the war in either direction.

THE BATTLE OF ALIWAL

Both sides received reinforcements before they met again on the battlefield. Gough had sent the second brigade of Smith's division, under Brigadier-General Wheeler, along with a regiment of native cavalry, the 400-strong Governor General's Bodyguard and four horse artillery guns. The march of Wheeler's troops caused Ranjodh Singh to withdraw from Bhudowal, fearing that he might get caught in a pincer. There was also a need to cover the crossing of reinforcements for his own army, so he would probably have withdrawn from Bhudowal in any case. Smith was able to occupy Bhudowal on 24 January and the troops took the opportunity to make their feelings known on the events of the 21st. Several villagers believed to have given assistance to Ranjodh Singh's men as they attacked Smith's column were killed and destruction was widespread. Colonel Roberts recalled how he and a comrade, needing to clean their clothes, had done so in a villager's house and then dried their garments by setting the house on fire.

At Bhudowal, Smith was also joined by the Shekhawatee Brigade, a combined cavalry and infantry unit, while Wheeler's men arrived on the 26th. Two 8in. howitzers added to his artillery, having been dragged by huge bullock teams from Ludhiana. On 27 January, Smith allowed his men to rest. It was a considerate gesture and one his men no doubt appreciated. It was also markedly different from the actions of Gough, who thought nothing

Photographed in 1858, it is just possible that one or two of the Gurkhas of the Nusseree Battalion pictured here may have fought at Aliwal. (SSPL/Getty Images)

of throwing his men into action at the end of a gruelling march. However, Smith's generosity was to have consequences, as 27 January also happened to be the day Ranjodh Singh received reinforcements to his own army.

Prior to this, although his force had been numerically impressive, the vast majority of it had been made up of irregular troops who could not be expected to stand in regular battle order. Now Ranjodh Singh was joined by 4,000 regulars, including men from Avitabile's Brigade. A further 12 guns were added to the Sikh Army as the reinforcements crossed in 50 boats at Tulwan Ford.

Ranjodh Singh finally seemed to be contemplating some sort of offensive, as his army was on the move on the morning of 28 January. It is uncertain what he had in mind, but whatever his plans were, they changed abruptly when Smith's army appeared on the scene. A defensive position was quickly taken up, the Sikhs arranging themselves in a perimeter roughly 2.5km in length, between the villages of Aliwal and Gorahoor, with their left flank reinforced by the village of Aliwal, in front of the main line. Ranjodh Singh placed his regulars, his steadiest troops, on his right flank, while the bulk of his 50 available guns were spaced out along the line.

The 4th Native Irregular Cavalry (known as 'Skinner's Horse') fought with Sir Harry Smith at Aliwal. Though not as disciplined as regular cavalry, irregular units could provide a valuable function as scouts or in pursuit of a defeated opponent. (Courtesy of the Council of the National Army Museum, London)

Smith had used his day of rest to organize his little army into brigades. He was advancing with his cavalry in front as a screen when scouts confirmed that the Sikh Army was on the move. Viewing the movements of the Sikhs from a vantage point in the village of Poorein, Smith determined to attack at once. As the Sikhs took up their hasty defensive positions, the British cavalry and horse artillery peeled away to left and right, revealing the infantry, marching in columns but already starting to deploy into lines, behind them. On the right of the line was Brigadier Godby with the Nusseree Battalion of Gurkhas and the 36th Native Infantry. Next came Brigadier Hicks' Brigade, comprising the 31st Regiment and the 24th and 47th Native Infantry. The two 8in. howitzers and 18 guns were massed in the centre of the line, before Wheeler's Brigade (the 50th Regiment, the 48th Native Infantry and the Sirmoor Gurkhas) continued the line. A further body of artillery, totalling 12 guns, came next, with Wilson's Brigade (the 53rd Foot, the 30th Native Infantry and the infantry of the Shekhawatee Brigade) completing the line on the left. The cavalry took up its position on the flanks, with the 1st and 5th Native Cavalry, the Bodyguard and the cavalry of the Shekhawatee Brigade on the right, while the 16th Lancers and 3rd Native Light Cavalry took station on the left.

Smith instantly realized that his line was overlapped on his right, so he reorganized slightly before giving the order to advance. Shortly after 10 a.m., the British line moved forward with skirmishers screening the main body. As the Sikh guns opened up, Smith called forward his horse artillery and

THE ADVANCE ON ALIWAL (PP. 70–71)

The 31st Regiment (1) is shown here advancing at Aliwal in a two-deep line, and has reached a distance of around 50 yards from the Sikh positions (2) based around a walled compound. The 31st wore white-covered, peaked forage caps, red shell jackets, with collars and round cuffs in buff, crossed shoulder belts and a haversack on the left hip, and white waist-belts (an item not normally worn by British regular regiments but adopted by East India Company regiments). A Sikh cavalryman (3) has bravely ridden out to confront the advancing British as the Sikh irregular infantry in the village desert their posts. A sword-armed British officer from the 31st (4) ran out to meet him, but before he could get there, the Sikh rider was shot from his horse. Some Sikh irregular troops can be seen in the village (5), holding their posts while others flee. Two Sikh artillery guns were located in the village at this stage of the battle (6), one of which (a 6-pdr) is shown here. The main Sikh defensive line lay to the rear of the village, about a quarter of a mile away (7).

an inconclusive duel carried on for around half an hour. Colonel Roberts again described the roundshot as coming at them like cricket balls, while an exploding shell prompted some of his men to open fire upon it, which triggered an angry reaction from Roberts. There was room for humour even under such stressful circumstances. Roberts recalled how one ball made a path through his men, knocking off a cap, smashing another man's arm and then cutting a haversack from a third man's back and spilling a loaf onto the ground. The soldier ran after his precious loaf as his comrades laughed.

Whether or not he had been able to discern which troops opposed him at the various points along the Sikh line, Smith now decided to throw the bulk of his strength at the right (as he looked at it), focussing on the village of Aliwal. By capturing it, his men would be able to enfilade the Sikh line. With Ranjodh Singh keeping his regulars grouped on the other end of his line, this meant that Smith would be attacking irregulars on this critical part of the battlefield. The brigades of Godby and Hicks were hurled at the village, taking it with little difficulty as it was only lightly manned, while the brigade of cavalry on the right flank kept Sikh horsemen at bay.

On the left, Wheeler's Brigade advanced steadily on the strongest troops in the Sikh lines. Under heavy artillery fire, they were twice forced to lie down, both to settle the men and to allow the supporting brigade, under Wilson, to keep up. British artillery also kept on the move to support the advance. The brigade of cavalry on Smith's left flank now moved into action. The 3rd Native Light Cavalry was first checked by Sikh horsemen, but the 16th Lancers then attained dominance and the Sikh position was fatally undermined.

The Sikhs were now forced to reorganize their lines, but Ranjodh Singh is believed to have already fled the battlefield by this point. With their left in tatters, they were nevertheless able to withdraw to a second line, based on

The 16th Lancers ride into the history books, charging Sikh artillery and infantry positions at Aliwal. The men of Avitabile's Brigade can be seen in a defensive formation in the background. Although the 16th Lancers are credited with breaking into an enemy square, the formation was actually a triangle. (Anne S.K. Brown Military Collection, Brown University Library)

the village of Bhundri. With no effective leadership, this was a remarkable achievement while under sustained attack and speaks to the quality of the Sikh soldiers. The Avitabiles in particular were causing problems when Smith once more ordered the 16th Lancers into action.

'The charge of one squadron of the 16th Lancers, led by Major Smyth and Captain Pearson, upon a well-formed square of Avitabile's Regiment, deserves special notice,' ran one account of the battle, 'as, notwithstanding the steadiness of the enemy, the Lancers broke the square, charged through, reformed and charged again in splendid style—a feat very rarely accomplished.' With the 53rd Regiment and 30th Native Infantry exploiting the success, and British horse artillery flying among the reeling Sikhs, the battle was all but over. A body of Avitabile's men attempted to make a stand, but were flushed from their position by the 30th Native Infantry, straight into the sights of 12 horse artillery guns. 'The destruction was very great,' Smith reported with grim satisfaction, 'as may be supposed, from guns served as these were.' The only question remaining was how successfully the Sikhs could disengage. Avitabile's troops remained steady despite repeatedly falling back, but elsewhere there was chaos as men clambered into boats, splashed through fords or simply hurled themselves into the river in an attempt to get to safety.

Aliwal has been referred to as 'the battle without a mistake', but while it is true it was well handled by Smith, it was not quite immaculate. The 16th Lancers, for instance, at one point came under fire from a regiment of native infantry, who thought they must have been Sikh as they were coming from so far behind the Sikh line (Colonel Roberts had flung himself before the troops, shouting 'Our men, our own men!' and lifting musket barrels with his sword). It is not known if this friendly fire had any effect on the

A particularly bloodthirsty image depicts the Nusseree Gurkhas in action at Aliwal, clearly intent on taking no prisoners. The Gurkhas' famed kukri knives can be seen. (Courtesy of the Council of the National Army Museum, London)

16th Lancers, but they did take the brunt of the casualties, with 59 officers and men killed and 83 wounded. They also lost 66 horses, with a further 35 being wounded.

Overall, though, Smith's casualties were remarkably light, thanks in his opinion to his army's 'bold and intrepid advance'. Only 151 men were killed in Smith's force, with 413 wounded and another 25 missing. Ranjodh Singh's army is believed to have suffered losses in the hundreds, but certainly less than the 3,000 estimated by the British after the battle. More serious was the loss of artillery. Every one of the guns Ranjodh Singh had brought into battle was either captured by the British or lost in the river. Smith was able to take 52 guns into his possession, as well as around 30 *jingalls* (small swivel-mounted guns, sometimes little more than heavy muskets).

Comparison is inevitably made between the leadership styles of Smith and that of Gough. The relatively light 'butcher's bill' run-up in securing a comprehensive victory at Aliwal has likewise been contrasted with the cost of the bloody actions at Mudki and Ferozeshah. The main difference in the handling of the armies on each occasion was the fact that Smith had allowed his men a day's rest before sending them into battle early in the morning on 28 January, and he took personal pride in the fact that he had not caused unnecessary casualties among his men.

The relief felt in British-occupied India at the news of the decisive victory was palpable. At the main British camp at Sobraon, Hardinge ordered a salute of cannon and the regimental bands played the national anthem. Curiously, reports suggest that strains of the same tune came from the Sikh bands on the opposite bank of the Sutlej. Smith was aware of how critically the campaign had been balanced at the time. 'The political importance of my position was extreme,' he noted. 'All India was at gaze, and ready for anything.' He was also aware of how easily things may have turned out differently. He was unsure of the quality of the leadership of Ranjodh Singh,

The Sikh artillerymen were again defiant in the defence of their guns, but Sir Harry Smith's force captured 52 of them, sending the majority back to the British base at Ludhiana. (Courtesy of the Council of the National Army Museum, London)

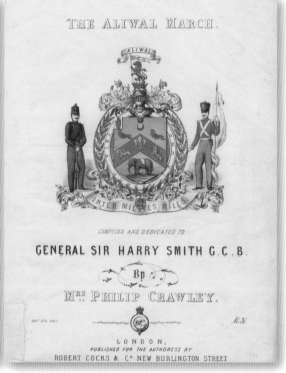

but still recognized his positioning to impede the march of the British to Ludhiana as most effective. 'It is the most scientific move made during the war,' he conceded, 'whether made by accident or design.'

Still, Ranjodh Singh had thrown away an opportunity to destroy Smith's straggling army at Bhudowal, and of then picking off isolated pockets of troops at will. The great siege train marching from Delhi would then have been an easy target. As things stood, the victory at Aliwal had completely changed the face of the campaign. Smith was gratified to hear from his political officer that the Sikhs had mostly withdrawn across the Sutlej. 'The position of the enemy at Sobraon,' Major Murchison reported, 'is now the only one held by the Sikhs south of the Sutlej.' As such, it would be the next target for Gough.

Smith was unable to move back to the main camp as quickly as he would have liked. The guns captured at Aliwal needed dealing with and that took time. He sent 47 captured Sikh guns to Ludhiana, using the transports of his own artillery for the job (most of the Sikhs' draught animals had been killed during the battle), and kept five of the most impressive pieces with his army. He was not able to start back towards Gough until 3 February. He left Brigadier Wheeler with a force to secure the area and marched with the 16th Lancers, the 3rd and 5th Native Light Cavalry, a corps of irregular horse, the 31st, 50th and 53rd Regiments, the 47th Native Infantry, the two Gurkha battalions and 200 wounded.

Four days later, Smith was welcomed enthusiastically by Gough. The commander-in-chief was in a good mood, not only due to Smith's success at Aliwal and his safe return, but because the first elements of the siege train from Delhi had arrived the previous day. His army was now the strongest it had ever been and he was ready to resume his campaign. The enforced period of inactivity had brought its own problems as well, as the camp had steadily descended into squalor and it was only a matter of time until the traditional camp illnesses erupted. Smith noted with distaste the state of the camp and quietly asked permission to move his men to a new location on 8 February.

The next day, he and the other divisional commanders were summoned to Gough's tent for orders. The details of the proposed assault did not impress Smith, as he believed the enemy was being attacked at its very strongest point. Gough's plan seems especially questionable given his knowledge of the inherent flaw in the Sikh lines, with its weak right flank. Smith's forebodings were to be borne out, as he made clear in a letter to his sister following the last battle of the war.

'Our last fight,' he confided, 'was an awful one.'

THE BATTLE OF SOBRAON

Soon after the Battle of Ferozeshah, the Sikhs had begun gathering boats to make a bridge across the Sutlej. This now joined their two camps, on the northern and southern banks of the river. The north bank was considerably higher, with the southern bank being a shallow sandy slope in many places. By 7 January at the latest, the bridge was complete, but it was initially used only for scouting parties and for spirited cavalrymen who wanted to indulge in a little skirmishing with British scouts. Over the remainder of the month, however, serious work was undertaken to set up a defensive position south of the river.

The British placed an advanced observation post at Rhodewala prior to the Battle of Sobraon, from where Gough was able to enjoy a clear view of the Sikh defences. (Anne S.K. Brown Military Collection, Brown University Library)

The line constructed by the Sikhs was strong in some places but perilously weak in others. Most notably, on the Sikhs' right flank the lines strayed into soft, sandy soil, which was unsuitable for extensive entrenchment. This was also the area left intentionally weak by Lal and Tej Singh. A system of river beds (*nullahs*) gave the Sikhs some natural defences to work with and some were incorporated into their lines, which stretched around 3km in total. The *nullahs* were mostly dry, although stagnant water was reported in the bottom of some.

The Sikhs were extremely vulnerable during this phase of their preparations, before they had shifted large numbers of troops across the river. While Smith was away on his detached mission, though, Gough had taken extra care not to antagonize his opponents. He did not have the ammunition necessary to seriously interfere with the work and did not want to trigger a spontaneous battle until Smith was back. In any case, the basic layout of the position was flawed, as Gough was well aware, and strengthening of the Sikh entrenchments was therefore allowed to continue.

The work was decidedly uneven. Some parts of the line had wooden ramparts around head height, while others had simple breastworks. Construction on the left of the Sikh position was under the command of Sham Singh Attariwala, an old but experienced general who knew his business and was not implicated in the treasonous correspondence with the British. Had he commanded the entire army, the war may have taken a very different course. As it was, he presided over the construction of the strongest part of the Sikh lines. Several British observers noted with some concern the quality of the works at this point.

As the line swung westwards, it became weaker. At the point where it shifted from roughly south-west to roughly north-west, the walls of the *nullah* along which the works were sited became shallower and the fortifications less ambitious. This became more emphasised as the line finally turned northwards, until only entrenchments and the occasional foxhole marked the defences. Weak as it was, it also failed to continue to the Sutlej, and the gap was plugged only by a cavalry force. Moreover, Lal Singh had placed irregular troops in this, the weakest part of his defences, and the lines here included no artillery. There could have been no clearer invitation to the British.

Some secondary, interior defences were constructed as well (including a series of deep pits that may have been intended to hinder the movement of cavalry), but none facing westwards to guard against British troops penetrating the right flank of the outer line. The entire position, therefore, could be undone by its built-in weakness. As well as the steady flow of intelligence from the Sikh camp, the British could use their own eyes, and it was clear there was no coherent plan behind the works. J. D. Cunningham, a British engineer, summed up the situation when he commented that 'the entrenchment showed a fatal want of unity of command and of design; and at Sobraon, as in the other battles of the campaign, the soldiers did everything and the leaders nothing'.

Two small outposts in front of the Sikh position allowed them to keep a watchful eye on the British while Gough recovered his strength and awaited reinforcements. Chote Sobraon, a small village about 2km south of the main defences, was one, while the second was nothing more than a tiny clump of trees, in which the Sikhs installed an observation platform. In return, the British could look into the Sikh position from their observation post at Rhodewala. Skirmishing and chance encounters between the two sides had punctuated the pause in hostilities, but as the day of battle neared, Gough put a stop to any such activity, unwilling to risk having men fall into Sikh hands and potentially divulge intelligence.

In the early hours of 10 February, the British troops were quietly awakened and moved into their positions for the assault. By 4 a.m., they were in place, less than 1km from the defensive works. Unlike his previous actions, at Mudki and Ferozeshah, Gough would not see this battle complicated by the setting of the sun. The British artillery was already in position and for the first time it outnumbered the Sikh guns, thanks partly to the consistent losses of artillery suffered by Tej Singh's army. An artillery barrage, it was hoped, would soften up the Sikh lines so that the assault would not be unduly costly. In fact, Hardinge had made it clear that he doubted the assault could work without such a barrage and had counselled Gough on the matter: 'If, upon the fullest consideration, the artillery can be brought into play,' he advised, 'I recommend you to attack; if it cannot, and you anticipate a heavy loss, I would recommend you not to attempt it.' The superior calibre of the Sikh guns had also been addressed to some extent. The siege train from Delhi had brought larger pieces and attempts had been made to increase a number of 9-pdr guns to 12-pdrs by boring out the barrels.

The Sikhs had an estimated 20,000 men in their lines south of the Sutlej. Almost all of their cavalry had been kept on the north side, as well as many

A colourful representation of the Battle of Sobraon, capturing the wide variety of units involved, from disciplined regular infantry to irregular cavalry. The attempts of the Sikhs to find refuge by crossing the Sutlej is also depicted. (Courtesy of the Council of the National Army Museum, London)

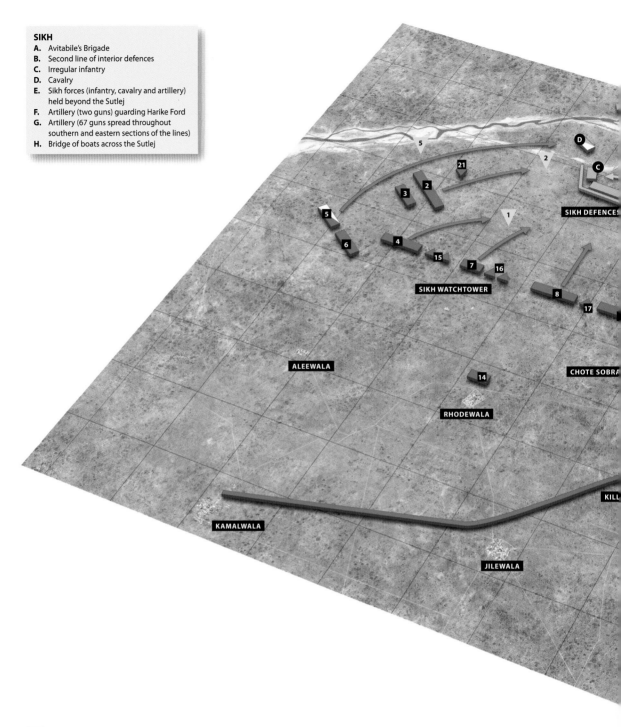

SIKH
A. Avitabile's Brigade
B. Second line of interior defences
C. Irregular infantry
D. Cavalry
E. Sikh forces (infantry, cavalry and artillery) held beyond the Sutlej
F. Artillery (two guns) guarding Harike Ford
G. Artillery (67 guns spread throughout southern and eastern sections of the lines)
H. Bridge of boats across the Sutlej

SIKH DEFENCE

SIKH WATCHTOWER

ALEEWALA

CHOTE SOBRA

RHODEWALA

KAMALWALA

KILL

JILEWALA

▼ EVENTS

1. The initial British artillery barrage is ineffective and short-lived, forcing the infantry to once more bear the burden of the assault.

2. At 9 a.m., on the British left, the heavily reinforced division of Sir Robert Dick makes steady progress against the weakest section of the Sikh lines, supported by three troops of horse artillery.

3. The Sikhs shift men to shore up their western defences.

4. The divisions of Sir Walter Gilbert and Sir Harry Smith stage a diversionary advance, but it is quickly turned into a full-scale assault.

5. British cavalry establishes dominance over its Sikh opponents on the left flank. Cavalry then penetrates the Sikh lines and enters the camp.

6. Smith's men attack the strongest section of the Sikh defences and are repulsed as many as three times before breaking through.

7. Around midday, the Sikhs begin to withdraw calmly, but the bridge of boats across the Sutlej has been weakened and thousands are killed or drowned while trying to escape.

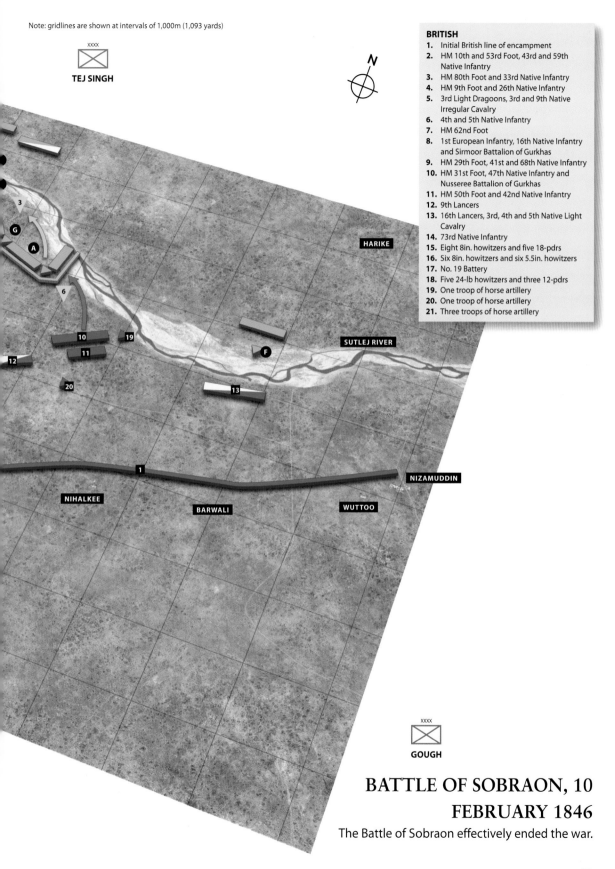

Note: gridlines are shown at intervals of 1,000m (1,093 yards)

XXXX
TEJ SINGH

N

BRITISH
1. Initial British line of encampment
2. HM 10th and 53rd Foot, 43rd and 59th Native Infantry
3. HM 80th Foot and 33rd Native Infantry
4. HM 9th Foot and 26th Native Infantry
5. 3rd Light Dragoons, 3rd and 9th Native Irregular Cavalry
6. 4th and 5th Native Infantry
7. HM 62nd Foot
8. 1st European Infantry, 16th Native Infantry and Sirmoor Battalion of Gurkhas
9. HM 29th Foot, 41st and 68th Native Infantry
10. HM 31st Foot, 47th Native Infantry and Nusseree Battalion of Gurkhas
11. HM 50th Foot and 42nd Native Infantry
12. 9th Lancers
13. 16th Lancers, 3rd, 4th and 5th Native Light Cavalry
14. 73rd Native Infantry
15. Eight 8in. howitzers and five 18-pdrs
16. Six 8in. howitzers and six 5.5in. howitzers
17. No. 19 Battery
18. Five 24-lb howitzers and three 12-pdrs
19. One troop of horse artillery
20. One troop of horse artillery
21. Three troops of horse artillery

HARIKE

SUTLEJ RIVER

NIZAMUDDIN

NIHALKEE

BARWALI

WUTTOO

XXXX
GOUGH

BATTLE OF SOBRAON, 10 FEBRUARY 1846
The Battle of Sobraon effectively ended the war.

of their heavy guns. Only 67 guns were made available to the southern defensive line, with the Sikh right flank having to make do with something like 200 *jingalls*.

Sir Harry Smith's division, of two infantry brigades, occupied the right of the British line, opposite the strongest portion of the Sikh lines. In personal correspondence and in his autobiography, Smith made it clear he did not appreciate tackling the Sikh lines where they were most formidable ('never catch a butting animal by the horns,' he noted in a letter to one of his sisters) but he added that he had no choice but to obey his orders. Horse artillery and a rocket unit supported Smith's men.

Gilbert's division of two infantry brigades occupied the centre of the line, with eight heavy guns between his men and those of Smith. Another, larger battery of guns (numbering 25, including 20 howitzers and five 18-pdrs) then divided Gilbert from the final division, under Sir Robert Dick. Targeting the weak point in the Sikh defences, Dick's men were to have the easiest of the day's fighting, and in order to maximize the weakness of this portion of the defences, Gough overloaded Dick's division. A first line included two British regiments, the 10th and 53rd, alongside the 43rd and 59th Native Infantry. A supporting line of the 80th Foot and 33rd Native Infantry followed, with a reserve comprising the 9th and 62nd Foot and the 26th Native Infantry. Behind these were cavalry units under Brigadier Scott (the 3rd Light Dragoons and 3rd and 9th Native Irregular Cavalry), as well as three more native regiments, the 4th, 5th and 73rd.

Gough's preparations, therefore, appear to have been sound, and if the artillery could do its job, Dick's division might roll up the Sikh lines at very little cost. As the British stood in their positions, the sun burned off the morning mist and the battlefield was revealed. Smith narrated in his autobiography how things started to go wrong almost immediately.

'At daylight,' he wrote, 'our heavy guns … opened fire, and with apparent success where the fire was most heavy, but to our astonishment, at the very moment of this success our fire slackened and soon ceased altogether.' Colonel Roberts, with the 31st Regiment in Smith's division, also noted how the artillery duel accomplished nothing. 'We were halted just out of range [of the Sikh guns] and a little to our left were the 9th Lancers. The enemy occasionally sent a long shot over their heads, and I remember distinctly watching how every man slightly bowed his head in his saddle as the shot whistled past, and all the pennons of the lances moved forward and then back again in the most perfect unison … After a short, far too short bombardment, which has been severely criticized since … the whole force advanced to the attack.'

Roberts' memory let him down at this point, or he may simply have been unaware of how the morning's events had played out. Gough actually sent Dick's division in first, intending to unhinge the Sikh position. It is true, however, that the preparatory bombardment was much shorter than ideal. It was also much shorter than planned, but a mistake appears to have been made, with the guns taking insufficient ammunition with them as they were moved into position before the attack commenced. The artillery exchange, however, had once more been inconclusive and with many of the Sikh guns well placed and protected by fieldworks, little impact had been made. After something like two hours, the British guns fell silent and Gough is reported to have exclaimed, 'Thank God! Then I'll be at them with the bayonet.'

Horse artillery now raced in front of Dick's division and began peppering the Sikh lines on the extreme right of their position. At 9 a.m., Dick's men began to advance. It was a steady, almost ponderous advance, as little was feared from the Sikh lines. With the horse artillery repeatedly advancing to keep in front of the infantry, they steadily closed on the weakest point of the defences. Personal accounts of the fighting at this point vary wildly and cannot be reconciled. Some claimed to have advanced into the teeth of a savage artillery bombardment, but the Sikhs had no heavy guns in that section of their lines and could only call upon their *jingalls* or the cannon sited on the opposite bank of the river. Other accounts are adamant that the advance was almost unopposed, with the 10th Foot walking through the defences with their muskets shouldered. It is far clearer what happened next. The Sikh soldiers in the rest of the lines, though lacking effective leadership, recognized the danger and began to rush to block the advance of the British troops. Guns in other parts of the line were also laboriously turned to face this threat, and some were able to enfilade the advancing British. Sir Robert Dick fell around this time and the assault faltered and was then repulsed.

Seeing the difficulties his men were in, and recognizing that the Sikhs were weakening their defences elsewhere to plug the gap on their right, Gough then ordered troops under Gilbert and Smith to advance to distract the Sikhs' attention from their right flank. At first, this advance was to be merely light infantry covered by artillery, but as it became clear the Sikhs were not sufficiently distracted by the diversion, and were in fact pouring more men over to their right to tackle Dick's division, Gough converted these demonstrations into full-scale attacks by the whole of Smith's and Gilbert's divisions.

The Sikh defences at Sobraon are breached by British infantry, although it is uncertain that the fortifications were as formidable as this painting would suggest. (Anne S.K. Brown Military Collection, Brown University Library)

Smith's men advanced into a maelstrom of defensive fire. Well organized in this section of their defences by Sham Singh Attariwala, Sikh soldiers were helped by dedicated loaders, allowing them to maintain a high rate of fire. Colonel Roberts reported advancing against works 12ft high (it is likely he was including the high banks of the *nullah*, upon which this section of the Sikh line was situated, in his estimate) and claimed to have been beaten back three times. Smith mentioned being repulsed just the once, and that because he had been forced to attack a section of the line he would have avoided if given latitude in his orders. To make progress, he was forced to skirt the lines towards the river and found a way through there, engaging the Sikhs in savage fighting. Smith rated the action as the most severe he had seen apart from Badajoz, New Orleans and Waterloo. 'Such a hand-to-hand conflict ensued, for 25 minutes I could barely hold my own,' he recalled. 'Mixed together, swords and targets against bayonets, and a fire on both sides. I never was in such a personal fight.'

In the centre of the British line, Gilbert's division had a similar experience. The defensive works where they first attacked were simply too high to be scaled and the men were forced back. Redirected to the left, to an area where the lines were much less formidable, the division managed to get into the Sikh position, although they needed to improvise, clambering over the backs of comrades to get over the parapet.

The Sikh line was now severely threatened, and there was little chance of a successful withdrawal. Gough's delay in attacking had not only allowed his men time to gather their strength, it had also brought the Sutlej into play. Its depth had increased significantly over the previous days, and fords that had once been manageable were impassable on the day of the battle. The bridge was the only way to safety, but with around 20,000 men in the camp, it would have taken hours for all of them to cross. The British were not about to give them hours, but the Sikhs also had another problem. Tej Singh, having fled the battlefield early on, had also destroyed one of the central boats supporting the bridge, greatly weakening it. On the opposite bank, he had placed artillery to cover the crossing, but was it there to prevent the British from making use of the bridge, or to punish any Sikhs who attempted to retreat? It is unclear whether or not these guns were actually used on retreating Sikh soldiers, but there seems to have been concern on their part that they would come under fire if they attempted to use the bridge to withdraw.

On the British right, Smith's men had moved inside the Sikh defences when they suddenly came under fire from behind. The Sikh guns in the works had been bypassed and their gunners had darted back in once the British had passed, manhandling the guns around and opening fire into the backs of the British as they continued their advance. A charge by the 50th Foot quickly retook the guns. Elsewhere, British cavalry had got into the Sikh position, through holes in the defensive works blown by British sappers. The cavalry had carefully picked their way through the debris, in single file, before reforming inside the lines and attacking the Sikhs there.

The battle now shifted into its last phase. Where there had been fierce fighting along the line, the Sikhs now mostly disengaged and walked calmly towards the river crossings. Colonel Roberts noted how he 'actually saw them marching (not running) with their arms sloped in the most defiant manner'. This quite remarkable display of bravery was repeated throughout the Sikh defences, but order inevitably broke down when the thousands of men pressed together at the bridge. British infantry calmly fired again and again into the retreating mass of men, while horse artillery set up to fire at close range. The shooting gallery appears to have continued until some soldiers were simply unable to bring themselves to keep firing against such a helpless foe. Inevitably, the bridge proved too weak to bear the weight of men on it and it collapsed, sweeping hundreds into the river. Elsewhere,

The bridge across the Sutlej collapses under the weight of men attempting to flee the British guns. The bridge had already been weakened by the fleeing Tej Singh. (Bettmann via Getty Images)

Sikh soldiers threw themselves into the water in an attempt to swim to the opposite bank, but few made it to safety due to the sheer crush of numbers. Sir Harry Smith noted how the Sikhs made a bridge of bodies across the river.

All the time, British muskets and cannon fired into the dense mass of struggling men, and still the Sikhs refused to ask for mercy. In fact, individuals would periodically charge the British with a sword or musket in hand, preferring to die facing their enemy than while trying to escape. In the heat of battle the British troops probably took little notice of the fact that the Sikh guns on the north bank of the river remained silent, but their passivity allowed the British to crowd the river banks and pick their targets with impunity.

No more than three hours after the men of Dick's division had begun their advance upon the Sikh lines, the Battle of Sobraon was over (Gough himself claimed it was done by 11 a.m.) and an estimated 10,000 Sikh soldiers had been killed. Once more the British had captured every Sikh gun in the position, 67 pieces falling into their hands. British losses were again severe, with 320 killed and 2,063 wounded. Smith coolly noted that his division's losses at Sobraon (635 killed and wounded out of a strength of just 2,400) exceeded the losses of his entire army at Aliwal. This time, however, the victory had been decisive and the Sikh Army's power had been smashed, at least temporarily. Gough noted the bravery of the Sikh troops during a battle he described, perhaps rather grandiosely, as the 'Waterloo of India'.

British troops cross the Sutlej on 10 February following their short, bloody and ultimately successful campaign. (Heritage-Images/TopFoto)

'Policy prevented my publicly recording my sentiments of the splendid gallantry of a fallen foe,' he commented, 'and I declare, were it not from a conviction that my country's good required the sacrifice, I could have wept to have witnessed the fearful slaughter of so devoted a body.'

The crushing defeat at Sobraon need not have signalled the end of the war. There were tens of thousands of uncommitted troops still available to the Sikh commanders, as well as hundreds of guns scattered through the state in various garrisons and forts. A powerful army could have been quickly assembled to continue the struggle, but that was never seriously considered. The aim of the Sikh leadership had been to weaken the army, if not completely destroy it, and this had been achieved. There was plenty of fight left in the men, but the authority of the army had been drastically undermined following four defeats in battle.

On 10 February, the British began to cross the Sutlej at Attaree Ford, near Ferozepore. The move, overseen by Sir John Grey, was unopposed and 24,000 men had crossed within three days. The army that had fought at Sobraon had been given a couple of days to recover and then marched to Ferozepore to cross the river, while Lal Singh kept the remnants of his army, including the troops that had remained on the north bank of the Sutlej at Sobraon, out of the way.

The Victorian appetite for musical pieces commemorating military victories continued with this piece in honour of the Battle of Sobraon, composed for the pianoforte. (Anne S.K. Brown Military Collection, Brown University Library)

Gulab Singh was placed in charge of negotiations for the Sikhs and reached the British camp on 16 February. He was not exactly greeted with open arms and the British continued their implacable march on Lahore, in battle order during the later stages as rumours of a Sikh army in the vicinity spread. Dalip Singh left Lahore to meet with the British on 18 February and returned to his capital with them on the 19th.

There was little to no negotiation in the talks that followed: British demands were simply met and the Treaty of Lahore was agreed on 9 March. A large swathe of land known as the Jullunder Doab was handed over to British control, along with all Sikh lands south of the Sutlej, while war reparations of 15 million rupees were demanded. The British knew full well that this vast sum could not be found and accepted Kashmir as part payment, immediately handing it over to Gulab Singh for his services (detailed in the 16 March Treaty of Amritsar), in return for 7.5 million rupees. The British also extracted permission to move armies through the Punjab at any time, slashed the strength of the Sikh Army to just 20,000 infantry and 12,000 cavalry and forbade the employment of European soldiers. The 36 guns that had avoided capture by the British during the short war were also confiscated.

AFTERMATH

Dalip Singh was escorted by British forces back to his palace at Lahore, having come out to meet the column marching on the capital. Negotiations were already under way to strengthen British influence on the Sikh state.

By the end of the year, Britain had tightened its grip on the former Sikh Empire via a third treaty, which gave a British resident in Lahore control over the operations of the state. A Council of Regency was set up, including two generals, Tej Singh and Ranjodh Singh, who had been defeated in battle during the war. Lal Singh, who had been reinstalled as *vizier* after the war but had since fallen out of favour with the British, was removed before the end of the year. Tej Singh made a much better job of clinging on to power, remaining as commander-in-chief of the army and amassing a vast personal fortune.

The weakened *Khalsa* was to prove problematic. Reducing the regular army to 25 battalions of 800 men each, along with 12,000 cavalry, cut its

paper strength down to 32,000, but the men dismissed from the service did not stop being soldiers overnight. They also nurtured resentment over their treatment and would be happy to rejoin the army if hostilities broke out again. They did not have long to wait.

The Sikh people had a hard time accepting that they had actually lost a war, or that the subsequent infiltration of the British was justified. The Sikh Army had crossed the Sutlej and been repulsed, but the people did not feel they deserved to effectively lose their independence as a result. The soldiers of the army were even more incredulous at the turn of events. Feeling (rightly) that they had been betrayed by their leadership, they remained defiant and convinced that they could have beaten the British if given a level playing field.

This resentment festered quietly for two years before it erupted into war once more. The fortified city of Multan became the focal point of resentment, as the British sought to install a Sikh governor (backed up by a British resident) to replace the Hindu governor Diwan Mulraj. When the newly appointed resident, Patrick Vans Agnew, was murdered along with Lieutenant William Anderson, a rebellion erupted that eventually led to open warfare. With the revolt starting in April, however, the British were both unprepared for a major campaign and unwilling to take the field before the weather cooled. Retaliation was therefore held back until November, at which point Sir Hugh Gough again led British and native regiments into action.

The young maharajah remained on his throne, supported by a Council of Regency and a British resident, until he was deposed following the Second Anglo-Sikh War. He spent the rest of his life in exile. (Bettmann via Getty Images)

The results were much the same as in the First Anglo-Sikh War, with Gough's army suffering casualties so high they led to questions about his fitness to command. After the costly Battle of Chillianwala, on 13 January 1849, in which Gough again attacked late in the day and sent his infantry forward into jungle, where they suffered heavy casualties in an inconclusive battle, Gough was officially removed from his command. Luckily for him, the order did not reach him in time and Sir Charles Napier was unable to take command of the army before Gough had exonerated himself with a decisive victory at the Battle of Gujerat (a lengthy artillery bombardment, which neutralized the Sikh guns, had paved the way to victory).

Defeat for the Sikhs in the Second Anglo-Sikh War led directly to the annexation of the Punjab. The empire that Ranjit Singh had worked so hard to construct had now lost the last vestiges of its independence, but the warrior ethos he had helped to create in his remodelled army would live on. Sikh units were to serve with great distinction in the Indian Army

Talks following the war were one-sided, with the British determined to dictate terms and no strong Sikh negotiator to take them on. On 16 December, a final treaty installed a British resident to oversee all aspects of the running of the state. (©TopFoto.co.uk)

The murder of a British civil servant (Patrick Vans Agnew) and a young officer (Lieutenant William Anderson) inside a fortified temple was one of the sparks that ignited the Second Anglo-Sikh War. (Anne S.K. Brown Military Collection, Brown University Library)

(which became the informal name for the armies of the three presidencies), in conflicts as diverse as the Indian Mutiny and both World Wars. The Sikh Regiment remains the most decorated regiment in the modern Indian Army.

The Battle of Chillianwala, 13 January 1849, was another in the long string of bloody confrontations overseen by Sir Hugh Gough, who was relieved of his command as a result. (Anne S.K. Brown Military Collection, Brown University Library)

Sikh soldiers were welcomed into the ranks of the Indian Army (as the armed forces of the three presidencies became known following the abolition of the East India Company) following the annexation of the Punjab. (Anne S.K. Brown Military Collection, Brown University Library)

Maharani Jindan had been exiled from the Punjab following the First Anglo-Sikh War and eventually moved to England to join her son, Dalip, who was removed from his throne following the annexation of the Punjab. The former maharajah converted to Christianity, having been raised very much as a British gentleman after his removal from power. He was taken to Britain in 1854 and made a favourable impression on Queen Victoria. In 1861, a reunion with his mother (by now prematurely aged, she died just two years later) rekindled his interest in his home state, but for the time being he remained in England, though he became increasingly agitated at what he now saw as the treacherous manner in which he had been deprived of his birthright. Having demanded redress from the British government, he set sail for India in March 1866, determined to return to the Sikh religion and, if possible, reclaim some of his lands and possessions. Unwilling to risk such a potentially troublesome presence in India, British agents intercepted his ship at Aden and he spent the last years of his life in France, dying in 1893 at the age of 55. His body was quickly returned to England and he was given a Christian burial at St Andrew's and St Patrick's Church at Elveden. Debate continues on whether he should be returned to his native land.

THE BATTLEFIELDS TODAY

Exhibits at the Anglo-Sikh War Memorial at Ferozeshah include weaponry from the conflict and four specially commissioned paintings by Kirpal Singh, depicting the four major battles of the war. (Ravi S. Sahani/The India Today Group/Getty Images)

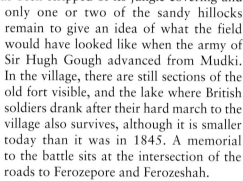

The battlefields of the First Anglo-Sikh War have been altered by time and the activities of the local population, but there are still interesting viewpoints to be enjoyed, as well as a handful of military memorials to mark the areas where the Sikhs contested the field with the forces of the East India Company.

The battlefield of Mudki has not been built over, although the village itself has expanded. The field has been stripped of its jungle covering and only one or two of the sandy hillocks remain to give an idea of what the field would have looked like when the army of Sir Hugh Gough advanced from Mudki. In the village, there are still sections of the old fort visible, and the lake where British soldiers drank after their hard march to the village also survives, although it is smaller today than it was in 1845. A memorial to the battle sits at the intersection of the roads to Ferozepore and Ferozeshah.

At Ferozeshah, the battlefield has been sliced up by new roads, canals and a railway line and new building has encroached into the area of the heaviest fighting, to the south of the old village. The explosions and fires after the battle completely destroyed the old village and nothing remains, but one of the many wells that surrounded the village (and which the British and sepoy troops crowded around after entering the Sikh entrenchments) survives. Monuments exist at Ferozeshah and Misreewala and there is also a museum dedicated to the war about 3km east of the village.

The villages of Aliwal and Bhundri have expanded considerably since they were the scene of fighting on 28 January 1846. The battlefield itself has also been levelled by farmers and most of the land is now cultivated, although several new villages

have also sprung into existence. The *nullah* that meandered across the area to the north of the original Sikh line still exists, however. A large battlefield monument also survives, although it is in a poor state of repair.

Canals and a dam have transformed the battlefield at Sobraon. In particular, it is now difficult to imagine the Sikh Army struggling to cross the Sutlej at the end of the battle as it is now extremely shallow and can disappear almost completely in the dry season. The changes to the river have also put paid to the ford at Harike, with the section that previously held two streams of the river reduced to a single, shallower one. Most of the entrenchments have disappeared over the decades, but in one or two areas they can still be made out, as the area has not been built upon. Some of the curious pits constructed within the Sikh lines can also still be made out. A British-built memorial remains in relatively good condition.

At Ludhiana, the Maharajah Ranjit Singh War Museum is comprised of multiple galleries, which deal with many eras of military history, including the Anglo-Sikh Wars. A diorama of the Battle of Aliwal is a particular highlight. Across the Sutlej, the fort at Phillaur, which has been turned over to the Punjab Police Academy, has been well preserved.

At Amritsar, a statue to Sham Singh Attariwala commemorates his heroic leadership at the Battle of Sobraon, where, dressed in distinctive white robes, he had rallied his men before dying on the battlefield. (Sameer Sehgal/Hindustan Times via Getty Images)

FURTHER READING

Several first-hand accounts of the campaign are available in print and online. Frustratingly, they often disagree about details both minor and major and it is often impossible to reconcile one with the other. The reader must make a judgement based on the weight of information and always bear in mind the possibility of a commander altering the tale slightly to cover up a mistake or exaggerate a success.

The War in India: Despatches (published 1846) contains the official correspondence of Hardinge, Gough and Sir Harry Smith, and is useful in the way it presents the campaign as it unfolds, rather than with the benefit of hindsight (after the Battle of Ferozeshah, for instance, Gough admitted to believing the war was over). More detail on Smith's exploits are given in his memoirs, *The Autobiography of Lieutenant General Sir Harry Smith* (1901), in which he is free of his criticism of Gough's generalship. The experiences of the most active regiment in the war, HM 31st Foot, are brought to life in the lively reminiscences of Colonel James Robertson in *Personal Adventures and Anecdotes of an Old Officer* (1906).

The war as a whole is well detailed in *The Sikhs and the Sikh Wars* (1897), by Sir Charles Gough (no relation to Sir Hugh Gough), although it has a distinctly British bias and the author was either unaware of the treachery at the head of the Sikh Army, or chose to ignore it. A more balanced consideration of the war, backed up with excellent detail on the battles themselves, is presented by Amarpal Singh in *The First Anglo-Sikh War* (2010). More detail on the formation of the Sikh state (including the dizzying period of intrigue following the death of Ranjit Singh) can be found in the second volume of *A History of the Sikhs* (1963, with a second edition in 2004), by Khushwant Singh.

For those interested in a closer consideration of various aspects of the war, a range of academic papers is available, including 'Recruitment and Reform in the East India Company Army', by Arthur N. Gilbert, 'Raja Gulab Singh's Role in the First Anglo-Sikh War', by Bawa Satinder Singh, 'Gulab Singh and the Creation of the Dogra State of Jammu, Kashmir and Ladakh', by Robert A. Huttenback, 'Military Developments in India, 1750–1850', by Pradeep Barua and 'Military Synthesis in South Asia: Armies, Warfare and Indian Society, *c.*1740–1849', by Kaushik Roy.

Finally, two Osprey books provide valuable detail on the two armies that met on the field of battle during the First Anglo-Sikh War. *The Sikh Army: 1799–1849*, written by Ian Heath and illustrated by Michael Perry, sits nicely with *Armies of the East India Company: 1750–1850*, written by Stuart Reid and illustrated by Gerry Embleton. A third Osprey title, *The First Afghan War 1839–42*, written by Richard Macrory and illustrated by Peter Dennis, includes details on the Sikh involvement in that conflict.

INDEX

Page numbers in **bold** refer to illustrations and captions and plates.